GREETINGS from MISSISSIPPI.

2015.

Chainsaws & Casseroles

A Collection of Short Stories & Cartoons

MARSHALL RAMSEY

From the Author of Fried Chicken & Wine and Banjo's Dream

Two-time Pulitzer Finalist

Chainsaws & Casseroles,

Published by Tiny Wheels Media, LLC

Dust cover and text layout designed by Tim Little
Illustrations by Marshall Ramsey

ISBN: 978-0-9883684-2-2
Printed in the United States of America

First Edition

marshallramsey.com
twitter.com/marshallramsey

TINY WHEELS
MEDIA, LLC

Dedicated to Amy, Daniel, David, Evan and Pip.

You've taught me that the worst moments are the seeds for the best.

Yes, even you, Pip.

THE MOMENT AMAZON REALIZED DELIVERY DRONES WON'T WORK IN the SOUTH.

Table of Contents

Foreword

It happened even before Hurricane Katrina's winds stopped blowing: We checked on our neighbors. Got gas (when we could find it) and bought stuff at the store. We then took the stuff to our church or synagogue. And we didn't just drop it off. We cut our way down Highway 49 to help our neighbors on the Gulf Coast.

When things got bad, we got good.

Sure, that's terrible grammar. But it's probably the truest statement I've encountered in my nearly 20 years of living in Mississippi. When the proverbial poop hits the fan, we rise to the occasion – and get busy helping those in need.

This book is born from that spirit and my speeches to thousands of Mississippians. It's a collection of essays, short stories and cartoons I've created over the past few years. If there's a golden thread that runs through its pages, it's overcoming adversity with humor and grit.

When a disaster strikes and before you can crawl out of the rubble, a church van will pull up full of people with chainsaws and casseroles.

That's who we are. That's what we're about.

Enjoy.

Marshall Ramsey

Acknowledgments

This book is a sum of a group of amazing people. At the beginning is my wife Amy. She's the center of my creative universe and the best mom, art teacher and spouse in the world. She met me when I was a high school janitor and knew I had potential (to clean the house.) Tim Little designed this and my first two books *Fried Chicken & Wine* and *Banjo's Dream*. All three prove he's brilliant at design – and he's a good friend. Joe White edited the stories and gave me encouragement – like he did for my editorial cartoons for over 15 years. He has a great used bookstore in Mendenhall, Mississippi; check it out. Speaking of bookstores, John Evans and Joe Hickman at Lemuria Books helped shape *Chainsaws & Casseroles* with their advice and friendship. I look forward to signing books in their fantastic bookstore soon. Mike Frascogna III's entrepreneurial spirit rubbed off on me, too. Pip the dog barked a lot while I was trying to write this. She's good at that and stealing socks.

But I really want to thank the good people of Mississippi. For 19 years, they've allowed me to come into their homes every morning. I've watched them time and time again prove my theory about becoming good when things turn bad. *Chainsaws & Casseroles*: It's more than a title. It's how they roll.

Chainsaws & Casseroles

A Collection of Short Stories & Cartoons

WHEN THINGS GET BAD, WE GET GOOD.
WE'RE HERE to HELP
AND FEED YOU.
FIRST UNITED

Chainsaws & Casseroles

Hail pelted the armored SUV nicknamed "The TANK." The driver nervously steered into the teeth of the storm while the navigator quietly examined the radar on his laptop. In front of them, a giant mile-wide wedge tornado thrashed across the Mississippi countryside.

"It's a MONSTER!" the driver yelled over the roar of the hail. "Look at that wedge! Check the map, Dr. Z. Are we headed the right way?!?"

Dr. Z, the navigator, looked over his reading glasses and calmly said, "Yes Mike. But I don't need a map. The tornado is headed toward Desoto Flats. It's my hometown."

Dr. Z, or Jimmy Zacharias, was the grandson of Greek immigrant Apostle Zacharias. Apostle had moved to Desoto Flats, Mississippi, after World War II and opened a hardware store. His son, James, inherited Zacharias Hardware when Apostle died of a massive heart attack. James' son, James Jr., was to take over for him. At least that was how it was supposed to be; however, James Jr., or Jimmy as everyone called him, loved the weather. He was fascinated by an old Indian legend that said the love and sacrifice of an Indian squaw for a European explorer protected Desoto Flats from tornadoes. Jimmy studied weather from the time he was a young child. A scholarship offer from the University of Oklahoma was to be his big break in to the weather business.

Except that his father would have nothing to do with it.

"Who will take over the business?!? I need you! I forbid you to go," his father screamed on that fateful August night.

"And you can't stop me," Jimmy yelled as he slammed the door in his father's face.

Those were the last words he had said to his father in over 25 years.

Jimmy excelled at meteorology. He graduated with a 4.0, earned his masters and then his doctorate. He specialized in tornado formation and spent many hours chasing massive storms on the Great Plains. His big break came when Hollywood producers approached him about a new reality cable TV show called "Tornado Hunters." An acting coach helped him lose his southern accent, a network executive suggested he change his name to Dr. Z and Hollywood created a cable TV legend.

Dr. Z was a star. And, like a star, he was lightyears away from Desoto Flats.

The Weather Network, a cable network based out of New York, hired Dr. Z to be its lead forecaster/storm reporter. Dr. Z's fame quickly rose even higher. If Dr. Z showed up in your neighborhood, you knew doom was not far behind. Dr. Z used his charm, scientific knowledge and rugged good looks to woo America and chase tornadoes.

Now he could do nothing as he chased one right into his old hometown.

"OMIGOD," he mumbled. His heart sank.

The TANK navigated through the downed trees, debris and fallen power poles. Dr. Z looked for familiar landmarks. None were to be found. The Pemberton Elementary school was gone. The Courthouse, built after Sherman had burned the old one, was leveled. Zacharias Hardware was gone. People walked in shock around the town square. It looked like a scene from "Walking Dead."

Mike pulled the TANK over and he, Dr. Z and the cameraman got out to render aid. People first, tornadoes second was their motto. Dr. Z watched as the tornado roared over the horizon. Judging by the apocalyptic damage, it had to be an EF-4 or 5.

Dr. Z pulled out his cell phone. No bars. He threw it down and then dug through the TANK for his satellite phone. He called his assistant in New York. "Jan, this is Z. We're in the middle of Mississippi. Tell the boss we need some aid sent down here. Tell him to pull some strings. Call the damned President. And tell the boss I'm also taking some time off. I have some work to do."

Jimmy looked around at what was left of Desoto Flats. God's finger, as he called tornadoes, had destroyed over 100 years of history in seconds.

Mike put a compress on an older lady's head. Dr. Z recognized her as Anne Smith, his old Sunday school teacher.

"Mrs. Smith," Dr. Z called out.

Mrs. Smith weakly muttered, "Jimmy?"

"Where are my parents?"

Mrs. Smith shrugged. "You seen my kitty, Jimmy?"

She was in shock.

Dr. Z ran toward his parents' house. The Victorian home had been built strong and had a storm cellar. He knew there was a chance his parents had survived. Bodies littered the streets. He pulled out the satellite phone again: "Jan, tell them there are mass casualties, too. WE NEED HELP!"

Dr. Z had lost his calm, cool demeanor. Even his southern accent started coming back.

He ran to the corner of Main and Stonewall Street looking for his parents house.

"MOM! DAD! MOM! DAD!"

He was silent for a second to hear any reply. The town was eerily quiet. The smell of pine burned his nose.

"MOM! DAD! MOM! DAD!"

He heard scratching coming from the storm cellar. It was covered with six-feet of debris.

Dr. Z started throwing boards out of the way. He then stepped on a nail which went through his foot, but the pain didn't stop him.

"MOM! DAD!"

Fifteen minutes later, he pulled open the steel door. There, in the darkness of the cellar, were his parents. All three broke down in tears. The Prodigal Son had come home.

As they walked back to the TANK, Dr. Z called out to his crew: "Hey! I want you to meet my folks!"

"You have parents?" Mike asked with honest shock. "You were actually born and raised somewhere?" Dr. Z had kept his past very private.

Now, though, he hugged the two people he had missed so much. "I'm sorry. So sorry."

Then a miracle happened. As the town crawled out of the rubble, church vans full of people with chainsaws and casseroles arrived to help Desoto Flats, Mississippi. Nature had done its best to knock the town down. But it was lifted back up by the compassion of strangers. Dr. Z smiled. Why had he run from this? Why had he been gone so long?

Dr. Z held his parents and smiled. The storms he had chased for years finally led Jimmy Zacharias back home.

I'm Thankful I Live in the Era of:

• Sneeze guards. Let buffet food's grossness stand on its own.

• Air conditioning: I bet the people in the 1800s smelled.

• Deodorant: See No. 2

• YouTube: My wife said she'd watch MTV all day to see a Duran Duran video when she was a teen (good luck finding a video at all on MTV). Now she can watch one as quickly as she can type in "Her name is Rio."

• Airplanes: Orville and Wilbur, you guys rock. Sure, airports kind of suck — but the whole experience of crossing the world in hours instead of months is awesome.

• Airbags. Not the kind that explode in your face randomly. But it beats the steel posts called a non-collapsable steering column that would impale our parents.

• Remote controls. Yes, son, when I was a kid, I was the remote control. I changed all three channels.

• Microwave ovens: Making leftovers better since 1946.

• Safety razors: Five safe blades > One scary-horror movie.

• The Internet. Teenage boys had to rely on *National Geographic* (um, for world knowledge.) Now you have the whole world tied to your phone. It's great for sounding smart at parties. And copious pictures of cats.

• Football. I'm still struggling with the whole concussion thing (because I had a few myself), but there is no better party than an SEC tailgate.

• Netflix: Binge watched "House of Cards" last night. Allows me to watch stuff when I want it.

• Modern dentistry: Novocain for the win.

• The Weather Channel. OK, showing my weather geekness here. But watching Jim Cantore in a hurricane is good TV.

• High fructose corn syrup: I hated being thin.

• GPS: Now when people tell me to get lost, I smile, and say, "Not possible."

• Tervis cups: No more sweating cups on the table.

• Ice Makers: Ice trays were the devil.

• Elevators. (Except for perfectly healthy people who take

them only one floor.)

• E-mail: I never would have gotten my million dollars from the nice man from Nigeria without it.

• Star Wars. I'll even forgive the prequels.

• Personal groomers. Trimming nose hair is now a snap.

• Soft-toilet paper. OK, toilet paper in general.

• Interstate highways. By-passing Mayberry's speed traps since 1956.

• Random lists on Facebook.

Falling from the Delta Sky

This is a sequel to the short stories "Above the Delta Sky" and "Beneath the Delta Sky" from the book *Fried Chicken & Wine*.

A tiny, lone yellow crop duster soared above the dark green fields of the Mississippi Delta. Its pilot pulled back on the plane's stick and finished its daily aerial ballet. The crops below were now sufficiently dusted; his day's work was done. He loved the flight home. It was when he could just let his mind go and fly. No worries about power lines or trees. It was just him and his Air Tractor 301. And Angie.

Angie was the love of his life, his wife and the mother of their son. Cancer had taken her physically from him years ago. But her spirit protected him every time he flew. He smiled as he looked at her picture taped to the instrument panel. Next to it was a picture of the only other girl who held his heart — their granddaughter Angie. She was named for the woman she so closely resembled.

And he had named his plane Angie, too. Some felt he loved the plane more than people. He wouldn't argue. Planes were more dependable than people anyway. Besides, he had aviation running in his veins — He had flown since he was a small boy. A long career in the military and commercial aviation had taken him around the world. But his family brought him back home to Mississippi. After a long estrangement, he and his son could now almost tolerate each other. Almost.

He smiled as he thought of his granddaughter. His mind drifted off again as the setting sun cast haunting shadows across the fertile land.

And then it happened.

Sputter. Cough. Sputter.

His mind snapped back to reality. The Air Tractor's Pratt & Whitney radial engine died. Its loud roar suddenly fell silent, turning the plane into a 7,800 lb. gliding brick. He had crashed twice in his life — once when he hard-landed his father's Piper Cub and rolled off the end of the runway. He spent most of his sophomore year in a cast after that adventure. The other was when he had nursed his shot-up A-1 Skyraider back to Pleiku Air Base in South Vietnam. Rescuers had pulled him unconscious from his burning aircraft. His arm looked like pork rinds from the painful burns. Now, he was about to experience his third crash.

He probably should have panicked, but he didn't have time. He spend his remaining seconds airborne looking for options. There weren't many, though. He was too low to the ground. His mind raced as he tried to figure out where he could put the plane down. To the left was a tree-line that he couldn't clear. To the right was the river. Straight ahead was another tree-line — but did he have enough altitude to clear it? On the other side of the trees was a soybean field. If he could just keep the plane from stalling...

The silence in the cockpit allowed him to hear his beating heart.

"Protect me, Angie."

"I'm going to make it," he thought as the plane grazed the tops of the trees. And he was almost right. But just as he reached the edge of the field, the landing gear snagged a giant oak. He heard the snapping of limbs and groan of metal. The plane flipped and fell like a stone to the waiting dark soil below. The pilot screamed as the plane tumbled and then crashed. There was a bone-crushing crack. Then blackness.

The yellow plane fell from the Delta Sky.

When he awoke, he felt the sting of blood in his eyes. What was left of the plane's crumpled cockpit was covered in his blood. He looked down at this arm. It was gray from his loss of blood. His eyesight began to blur. He looked down at his leg and saw his femur sticking out of his pant leg. The world went gray and then black. Then he saw a brilliant light.

He had seen specials about near-death experiences and figured that he must be having one. He was wrapped with a peace like he had never felt before. And then he saw her. Glowing brightly with white flowing robes, Angie came out of the light. She was more beautiful than he remembered. She looked as she had the day they married. He heard her voice, yet her mouth did not move.

"Will you stay here or come with me?"

This was the moment he had dreamed about for years. He had been tempted to fly his plane into the ground many times just so he could see her again. So he could get this choice. Now he had gotten it. He started to head toward the light.

But he could see little Angie, too. He could see her crying at his funeral. He saw her flying to be closer to him. She saw her marriage. Her baby boy named for him. He saw the life he'd miss if he died.

And then he looked back at the love of his life. He felt her warmth radiating from her glow. He felt a peace he had not felt in so many years. His heart melted thinking of her love.

Then saw little Angie again.

He made his choice.

— — — — — — — —

He opened his eyes again and wasn't familiar with his surroundings. He blinked, tried to adjust to the whiteness of the room and then heard beeping and whirring.

"He's awake. Daddy, Grandpa's awake."

"I thought we had lost you, old man." His son looked down at him. "And as much as this might shock you, I'd have been devastated. I know Angie would have been, too. She needs her grandfather. I mean, c'mon — who will teach her to fly?"

"Oh, and sorry about your plane. There's not much left of it — but that was a heck of a piece of flying you did, dad. Doctor said it was nothing short of a miracle that you survived the crash. Your guardian angel was working overtime, that's for sure."

The pilot then saw his wife's spirit standing in the corner of the hospital room. He began to talk quietly under his breath. "I'm sorry, honey. I promise I'll spend eternity with you. But right now, our little girl needs me. I know you understand."

His wife nodded quietly and turned around. She faded into mist, revealing a little girl standing at the foot of his bed.

"I'm glad you're OK, grandpa."

"I'm better than OK," he rasped. "I'm with you."

For years he dreamed of seeing and being with his beloved Angie again. But he made the choice to keep on living.

All after falling from the Delta sky.

Meet Pip

Late that horrible Saturday night, my family and I walked into our now-empty house and were crippled by the pain of Banjo the dog's death. At that moment, we vowed to take some time between dogs. We were emotionally (and financially) drained.

I picked up the phone the next day and called Vicki, the breeder who had given us Banjo (as a rescue). When he died, he was the last Calirose Border Terrier living. Her dogs were and had produced a distinguished string of champions. Banjo wasn't one of them. But he was champion when it came to having heart. I told her the bad news about his death and thanked her profusely for allowing Banjo and Molly (our other Border Terrier who died in November 2010) into our lives.

A few days later, Vicki let us know that a friend of hers, Jim, had a Border Terrier who had a litter of pups. We told her we'd think about it and would let her know. But then she said, "They were born right about the time Banjo died." The coincidence was too much.

Our plans to wait a year between dogs shrank to weeks. But it wasn't a bad thing. My wife and I hadn't gone a day without saying, "We miss Banjo."

Sometimes you don't find a dog. Sometimes the dog finds you.

Pip came home yesterday. She's the smallest of the litter – not a runt, but small. Jim started calling her Pip for Pipsqueak and it stuck. She also was the most alert and first to greet Jim when he came to the box to check on them. She walked into our home like she has been in it for years and loves to play with all three of my boys. She's pretty much house trained and loves to cuddle with my wife. She's mostly black right now, but will lighten up like her mother Twinkee as time goes on. (Her father, Rocky, has black fur). Her mother was incredibly smart and by all indications, she is a chip off the old block. It is going to be a fun ride.

We still miss Banjo. Like I've said so many times before, he was a special dog. But I know Pip will be special, too. Talking to Jim yesterday, I found out that Pip was born nearly at the same moment Banjo died. I don't know if any of Banjo's spirit got into this feisty little girl. But I'd like to believe it did.

YOU INSTALLED THE DEER WHISTLES BACKWARDS.
CHEVROLET
MARSHALL RAMSEY

The Lizard

Somewhere near Destin, Florida, sits an old man who paints heaven after living through hell.

They call him the Lizard. Every day, he rolls his wheelchair down the dock and every day, he quietly paints as he soaks up the sun. The workers at the marina had a pool to guess his identity, but no one really knew for sure. All they knew was that he was old and didn't speak and had been painting on that dock for as long as they had been alive.

As the Lizard quietly applied watercolor to canvas, a slight breeze rippled the clear water. Cumulonimbus clouds exploded on the horizon. Storms would be there by noon. But that didn't seem to bother the Lizard. He just continued to paint.

A gull landed on a post nearby. The Lizard stopped what he was doing and pulled a crust of bread out of the tackle box. He tossed it to the waiting bird. It seized the crust and flew off. It was a routine the two practiced every morning. The Lizard wished he could be so free.

Instead, he continued to be a prisoner of a war that ended many years ago.

In an attempt to be released, he had painted over 500 paintings since the end of World War II. That war. The war that cost him his soul.

A sergeant in the Marine Corps, the Lizard had been in a foxhole on some Godforsaken South Pacific Island. A Japanese late-night sneak attack cost his best friend's life. The Lizard was on watch and had fallen asleep. For reasons he didn't understand, the Japanese infiltrators had spared him.

He wished he had died that night.

The next day he tried to commit suicide by charging a Japanese machine gun nest. Instead of death, he received the Congressional Medal of Honor.

The last time the Lizard spoke was when he gave the medal to his best friend's parents. His last words were, "I'm so sorry." That was in 1946. The next day, he walked away from his parents' home and disappeared into the night. He took his Marine Corps back pay and bought a small piece of land on the Gulf Coast. Then he picked up a brush and tried to make peace with God.

Everyday, he prayed, "Release me from this pain. Let me

die on this dock."

But God had other plans. One day, a rich yacht owner saw one of the Lizard's paintings. While reluctant to sell at first, the Lizard wrote an obscene number on a piece of paper — and the crazy, rich fool bought it. The old man held the check in his hand and felt the Holy Spirit plant a seed of an idea into his head.

Today, the V.A. Outpatient Clinic at Eglin Air Force base has a secret benefactor. Returning warriors from Iraq and Afghanistan receive extra care and help. And those suffering from PTSD have an angel watching out for them.

An angel named the Lizard — just an old man painting heaven after suffering through hell.

The New Passenger

I pulled our silver Maxima to the hospital's front door and put it in park. I got out to open the back door. My wife handed me our newborn son and I gingerly put him into the car seat. "I sure hope I installed this darn thing correctly," I thought as I buckled him in. Then I helped my wife into her seat and put her luggage into the trunk. I walked around the car and got in, turned the key and looked in the mirror.

There, turned rearward, was my son. My child. My firstborn.

I have never felt such euphoria and fear at the same time. "What do I do now?" I thought. I looked right and left and right again as I prepared to pull out into traffic.

For the first time in my life, I was truly responsible for another human being. "Please don't let me screw this up," I prayed.

I drove UNDER the speed limit all the way home.

Fatherhood didn't come naturally to me. Still doesn't, to be honest. But I accept now that kids are tougher than I thought that day. I wish they came with instruction books stapled to their butts. They don't. Each of my sons requires me to be a different dad.

But my first son was my education. And 15 years after his birth, I think I figured out the secret – give them copious amounts of time and love.

I had all three boys in my car today as we drove near Dogwood. Traffic was horrible and I looked in my mirror again. I realized I had precious cargo in my car. I started to feel that same feeling again. And then I smiled.

If I could go back to that day when we pulled away from the hospital, I'd tell myself to relax and enjoy the ride.

The Lizard – Part 2

It was a typical lazy Wednesday in Destin.

The hot, subtropical sun beat down on the dock, causing a bead of sweat to trickle down the old Marine's nose. It was noon, and the Lizard once again sat in his wheelchair painting Choctawhatchee Bay. He watched as a pelican slid gracefully across the water, gliding until just the right moment before crashing headfirst into the water. "There has to be a better way to get lunch," the Lizard thought. Why couldn't they just order from the snack bar? The Lizard had lived on fried food for nearly two decades.

"I might not live to be 100 if I keep this up," he chuckled to himself.

Ominous clouds built from the southwest. It was hurricane season and storms blew up quickly this time of year. The water was as warm as bathwater and the Gulf was like a fireworks tent run by chain smokers.

But he didn't care. He had survived several storms — here and on Okinawa.

His leathery fingers flexed as he carefully packed his paints and took the canvas off the easel. Thunder roared as he rolled up the dock toward the Cranky Pelican's snack bar. Joe, the owner, knew the Lizard ate fried shrimp and oysters everyday for lunch. And like every other day, Joe had it waiting with a cold beer.

The Lizard nodded and put down his money. Joe offered to run a tab, but the Lizard was a child of the Great Depression. He didn't believe in debt.

Lightning struck one of the condo towers across the bay and rain began to pelt the Cranky Pelican's roof. Lobster-red tourists ran for cover as wind whipped the snow-white sand into a swirling tempest. Tables overturned and chairs scattered. The Lizard laughed. In his younger days he would have welcomed God to strike him down.

But not today. He had work to do.

The Lizard needed to complete his painting. The wounded warriors at the V.A. needed his help.

A strange sound came up from behind, catching him by surprise. It was too heavy for footsteps. He turned quickly to see a brown-headed man behind him. The Lizard looked down and saw two prosthetic legs.

"I hear you're a good painter. Mind if I join you?"

The Lizard nodded.

"I also hear you're a crappy conversationalist. No worry — I'll do the talking."

The Lizard smiled. He hadn't spoken in nearly 70 years. Some people said he had forgotten how to talk. The last words he had said were "I'm so sorry" to the parents of his best friend — a friend who was dead because of him. Guilt and pain took his voice. The Lizard could still talk – he just didn't want to.

"My name is Randy. Like you, I'm a Marine. I proudly served in Baghdad. And I think my legs are still back there. Anyway, I want to paint with you."

The Lizard looked closer at Randy's arms. He could see scarring where shrapnel had torn his flesh. This boy had gone through his own brand of hell. The Lizard pointed to his canvas and nodded.

"Great! But first, let's eat," Randy grinned.

The Lizard watched as the young man wolfed down his oysters. Another bolt of lightning hit close by, rattling the liquor bottles at the bar.

By the time Randy's plate was clean, the rain had subsided. The Lizard rolled out to the end of the dock. Gray clouds shrouded the bay. Randy pulled up a chair and put a canvas on his own easel. Both men silently looked out on the bay and waited as the clouds began to clear.

"I came home from the war a wreck. I lost my job, started drinking and then my wife left after I became violent. I looked for answers in the bottom of a bourbon bottle. Didn't find them. Then I went to the V.A. and got counseling. They said I could get additional help because of an anonymous benefactor. One day as I was walking out of counseling, I saw the most beautiful painting I had ever seen. It was in the lobby. So I went to the art store and bought some canvases. My first painting was a mess. But the second one was a little better. And then the third was even better. Soon, I felt peace while painting. I asked who painted the painting in the lobby, and someone told me about you. The men at the marina said I'd find you here. They said people called you the Lizard and you didn't talk.

"Well, since you don't talk, you don't have to say 'You're welcome.' But I will say this, 'thank you.' You saved my life. And my marriage. And my soul."

Both men stared at each other for a moment and a tear trickled down the Lizard's cheek. He reached out his hand and shook Randy's scarred hand.

Then he looked him in the eye and spoke his first words in seven decades.

"You're welcome, Randy. My name is Bob."

At that moment, the warm Florida sun broke through the clouds, illuminating both men.

The storm was over. And the Lizard finally found peace.

Ten Random Things I Love about Being a Dad

With Father's Day coming up, I thought I'd jot down 10 random things I love about being a dad.

10. Watching the kids sleep. Sure, it's the least stressful moment of parenthood, but there's something remarkably magical about watching their little chests rise and fall with each breath.

9. Chest-swell-with-pride time. Straight As, athletic achievements, etc. You know the drill. Those good times that recharge your patience after you have to snake the toilet because of toys down the drain or pull gum out of the dog's fur.

8. The first time your kid greets you at the door when you come home from work. Nothing quite like it. You feel like you've liberated Paris during World War II. "DADDY!!!!"

7. Stories at bedtime. One time, I awoke to my youngest son poking me in the forehead. I had fallen asleep while reading "Goodnight MOON!"

6. The first time your kid says, "I love you, dad."

5. Throwing ball with your kid. Actually, any time you spend with them. It can be boogie boarding, grass cutting, house painting or car washing. Riding horses or bike, hiking or doing homework. It's about time. All about time.

4. A potty-trained child. No more diapers? It's a raise.

3. When your kids make you laugh — intentionally or unintentionally. In our house, love = humor.

2. Childbirth. Realizing you had a part in creating an amazing new life (and all the terror that comes with it.)

1. The privilege of watching them grow up.

I PLEDGE ALLEGIANCE to the CUP THAT HOLDS MY CAFFEINATED BEVERAGE. AND to the DRINK WHICH IT CONTAINS, ONE CONTAINER, FULL OF COFFEE, INDISPENSIBLE WITH ENERGY and CAFFEINE FOR ME!
MANNA
MARSHALL RAMSEY

Revenge of the Football Gods

In the South, there are two types of religion. In one, the faithful worship in churches on Sunday. And in the other, fans worship the football gods in stadiums on Friday and Saturday nights. It's a religion based on pride, violence and achievement. And one of its biggest gods was an 18-year-old quarterback from the small town of Cochran, Mississippi.

Tommy Lawrence stood over 6'5" tall. He had blonde hair, blue eyes and very little body fat — in fact, he looked like a football god. He had a big smile and a laid back personality. The son of an accountant and a kindergarten teacher, he was an unlikely success story. Playing his very first game as a Junior, Tommy was now on the cusp of leading the Cochran Bears to their first state championship one season later. Scouts from Alabama, Oregon, Ohio State, Tennessee, Ole Miss and Mississippi State practically lived with the family. Tommy Lawrence had a very bright future.

One strange thing about Tommy was that no one had ever seen his father, Thomas Sr., at one of his football games. His mom, Sue, sat faithfully in the stands, wearing a big button with Tommy's picture on it. But his dad was nowhere to be found. Thomas Sr. was a mild-mannered man who seldom raised his voice. The only time anyone had heard him angry was the night when Sue put her foot down and screamed, "I don't care, Thomas — Tommy is not going to carry your baggage. He is going to use his God-given talent and play ball." The neighbors could hear Thomas Sr. yelling a block away.

For two seasons Tommy had looked for his dad in the stands and for two seasons, he wasn't there.

The morning of the big game, Tommy confronted his dad. "You will be there tonight, right?" His father just grumbled and grabbed his briefcase. Tommy repeated louder, "YOU WILL BE THERE TONIGHT, RIGHT?!?"

Thomas Sr. turned quickly and glared at his son. He then screamed, "YOU DON'T UNDERSTAND!" Tommy picked up an old trophy off the bookshelf and threw it at the door where his father had just exited. The brittle trophy shattered like broken dreams as it hit the wall.

"You're right," Tommy mumbled. "I don't understand."

His mom walked out of the kitchen and said, "Don't be so

hard on your father. He has a very good reason for not wanting to be there."

"Why don't you share it with me, then," Tommy snarled.

"As soon as you drop that tone."

Tommy walked over to his mom, hugged her and said, "Sorry." He then sat down on the couch as his mother began to tell the tragedy of Thomas Sr.

"Your dad was as good as you were, if not better. He started his Freshman, Sophomore and Junior years. And then Coach Papa Bull was hired."

"Papa Bull? He's the coach of the team we're playing tonight."

"That's right. And he was a monster to your father. No one is really sure why. He said your dad was cocky and overrated. And he wanted his son to play quarterback. He'd tell your dad he was no good, would bench him randomly. He had to do extra conditioning. He rode your father and tried to make him quit. He verbally abused him every practice."

"What did grandpa do about it?"

"Nothing. Your grandfather was a workaholic. He was never there to defend your dad. Anyway, one practice, right before the biggest game of your dad's Junior season, Coach Bull shoved your dad down on the ground. Your dad snapped and came back up off the ground and Coach Bull punched your dad in the face."

"OMIGOD."

"It gets worse. Coach Bull forced the players and the other coaches to take his side. Even your dad's best friend Matthew was forced to lie by the coach. Your dad got expelled. So his family had to move to another school district. Your dad never played football again. In fact, he has never stepped foot in another stadium. This is hard on your dad, Tommy. Cut him a little slack."

"Yes, ma'am."

Tommy picked up a piece of the broken trophy. It read, "All-State Team, 1986 Thomas Lawrence." He put it in his pocket.

He vowed to get revenge for his father.

The setting sun cast an orange glow in the sky over Memorial Stadium in Jackson. Colorful signs read, "We love you Papa!" "Win Papa's Last GAME!" "Win one for the PAPA." "One last retirement gift for the PAPA!" Tommy felt his stomach churn as he saw the huge coach standing on the other sideline. He knew the coach knew his name. Now it was time to show him who he was.

And for three quarters he did just that. Tommy chewed up the Gaffney Giant's vaunted defense. The score at the beginning of the fourth quarter was Cochran 28-Gaffney 7. But Coach Papa wasn't going to be denied his last State Championship. He started sending in blitz after blitz. And he told his players that there would be a bounty for the first one to put Tommy out of the game. Tommy got punched in the groin. He got his eye gouged. Blood trickled out of his nose. With two minutes left in the game, Gaffney tied it 28-28.

Tommy looked over at the opponents' coach and mouthed, "I'm taking you down, you son of a….."

And then he did it.

Sportswriters call it "The Drive." Although there were 22 players in action, one person singlehandedly moved the ball 100 yards down the field. The football gods couldn't have touched their chosen son. With no time remaining, Tommy ran a bootleg into the endzone and scored the winning touchdown.

Coach Papa Bull had fallen at the hands of the son.

As the two teams mingled on the field, Coach Bull walked over to Tommy. "You have more courage than your old man. But you're still nothing. You're a loser."

Tommy said, "Get away from me, coach. I said what I needed to say on the football field."

And then, without warning, Coach Bull punched Tommy in the face, knocking him down.

Before Coach Bull could turn around, he felt a crushing blow against his chin. He saw a flash and then hit the field face first. As Bull faded in and out of consciousness, he heard a voice he had not heard in 27 years.

"You don't hit my son."

Tommy swung around to see his father standing over his old coach.

He ran over to his father and nearly knocked him to the ground. "YOU CAME TO THE GAME!"

His dad just smiled and put his arm around his son. "I

wouldn't have missed it for the world."

And as the two men walked off the field together, the football gods smiled.

Thanks Fannie

On the way to work, I stop and buy an unsweetened iced tea at the Whataburger on High Street in Jackson. And when I do, I'm greeted with an infectious smile and warm hello by a worker named Fannie. I don't know much about Fannie other than the fact that I'd hire her in a minute if I owned a business. In this age of mad fast-food workers (except Chick-fil-A's 'My pleasure' crew), it's pretty darn refreshing.

This morning was different, though. You could almost see the black cloud hanging over her head. I don't know what was going on, but SHE was not happy about it. I felt like I was in some kind of bizarro universe.

I took a second, paid my money (she automatically knows what I want and still tries to up-sell me!) and said all I could say:

"Every morning I come in here, you make my day. I appreciate you, your smile and the great service you provide."

Her face lit into a smile.

It wasn't much of a gesture on my part. But if I gave Fannie a few seconds of happiness, my debt to her is partially repaid.

Mrs. Ethel

Logic said go one way, his car's GPS said the other. Mike Goodall listened to the GPS pleasant female voice and now was hopelessly lost in the Mississippi Delta. He thought he was in Leflore County, although he was actually in Holmes County. It was night, and even his headlights couldn't burn through the deep, impenetrable Delta darkness. There was no moon. No stars. And now, no gas in his car's gas tank.

His low fuel light burned ominously on the dashboard. Mike looked down at his cellphone. It had bricked 20 minutes ago. And, of course, his wife had the car charger in her van.

"I'm toast," Mike thought. The last gas station he had seen was in Greenwood. He scanned the horizon — nothing. Until...

It was faint and barely a pinprick on the horizon. The small light looked like a third-rate star battling to be seen in the dark night sky. But it was definitely a light. Probably a house. And hopefully a phone.

A song called *Faster than Light* by Neil Finn played on the car's stereo. Finn, the front-man for the band Crowded House, had come out with a fantastic solo album in 1998. A particular lyric caught Mike's ear,

"And praise will come to those whose kindness
leaves you without debt
And bends the shape of things
that haven't happened yet."

Mike laughed. It seemed particularly naive. But at this point, he would take any kindness he could find.

He turned right onto a gravel road that led toward the light. A quarter of a mile later, he discovered the light belonged to an old white house partially obscured by four trees and a handful of rose bushes.

It was 10 p.m. He hoped someone was awake. Otherwise, he was stranded for the night.

Mike switched off the ignition. He opened the door slowly and got out, hoping there weren't any yard dogs. So far, no barking. So far, so good.

The house's door open quickly and a shotgun barrel popped out of the door. The gun discharged over his head, tearing at the branches and causing Mike to pee a little in his suit. "HOLY

CRAP!" he screamed.

An older feminine voice said, "WHO GOES THERE? I HAVE A GUN AND AS YOU CAN SEE, I AIN'T AFRAID TO USE IT ON YOU!"

Mike used as much respect as he could muster, "Ma'am, my name is Mike Goodall and I'm a vice president of a major company in Jackson. My car is out of gas and I was hoping to use your phone."

Silence greeted his words. He watched the barrel of the shotgun closely before it slowly lowered.

"You don't seem like one of those robbers that keep stealing my stuff."

"No, m'am. You mind if I come in to make that phone call?"

"C'mon in, boy. My name is Ethel Johnson. And, yes, you may use my phone."

As Mike was heading into the house, he looked around the yard. It was dark, but he could see a rusted-out old Camaro and an old Ford pickup truck. A broken-down tractor and some rusty farm equipment were sprinkled near a collapsing barn. Off to the left was a shed. He was sure that the owners of this homestead had once farmed this land heavily by themselves. Now, most of the surrounding land was corporate owned. Ethel probably leased the rest of what she had left to help pay her bills. By her looks, she was 85. And, apparently, she lived alone.

Mrs. Ethel shuffled and held the door open as Mike slipped inside. A hot blast of wind hit him from the inside. She apparently liked the house to be as hot as a summer afternoon on the planet Mercury. Three space heaters glowed bright as the sun.

"Mah phone is over there, son." Mrs. Ethel pointed to the rotary phone on the table. "I hope your number is an 800 number. I ain't got long distance. I don't have any family left and there is no one outside of the area I particularly want to talk to. No need to pay Ma Bell any more than I have to."

"I think it will be OK, m'am." Mike called the number on the back of his AAA card.

"They said it would be about an hour before they could get the gas here. You OK if I sit in here with you?"

Mrs. Ethel smiled. She appreciated the company. "Haven't had anyone to really talk to since my cat died last year."

Mike smiled and sat in the old chair by the door. An old tube television sat glowing in the corner. And the single light that had been his beacon burned warmly overhead. Mrs. Ethel brought two glasses of sweet tea

"You got family, son?"

"A wife and two kids. About to get a divorce, though. Wife and I just can't get along any more."

Mrs. Ethel cringed as she set the glasses down. "You don't want to do that. You don't want to be alone like Mrs. Ethel."

Mike smirked and than said, " You don't understand. She's impossible to live with."

Mrs. Ethel smiled and said, "And I'm sure you're a regular Prince Charming. You need to love on that woman, Mr. Mike. Your marriage is like a bank account. I bet you're completely overdrawn. Make small deposits — not because you have to, but because you want to. Don't expect anything in return. Your two children will appreciate it in the long run."

Mike nodded. He knew the old woman was right. But his pride was in his way.

Ah, his pride. It was why his life was in the mess it was. Mike was a proud man. He had built an impressive career against the odds. Nothing had come easy for him. He was consistently having to prove others wrong. Therefore, he had a huge chip on his shoulder.

A crash outside caused him to turn quickly.

"The thieves are back"

Mrs. Ethel grabbed for her shotgun. Mike cut her off, "I'll take care of this. Call the sheriff."

He went out the back door and snuck around to the side. There he saw two kids rifling though Mrs. Ethel's shed. Then they started heading toward the house. The only thing standing between them and Mrs. Ethel was him.

He saw a kid raise a pistol toward the old lady. Without thinking, Mike leapt between then and as the gun went off, Mike felt a searing pain in his arm. He hit the ground, aimed the shotgun and took two quick shots, hitting both thieves. Both clutched their own arms and ran off into the night.

"That was the most amazing, giving and unselfish act ever. And you've only known me for an hour. Now try that with the wife you've built a life with. Show that kind of love and caring for her. "

Mrs. Ethel touched Mike's wound and like vinegar on baking soda, a white foam began to cleanse the bullet hole. As the pain faded, he looked down and noticed that the wound and blood were completely gone.

"Who are you?"

"A light in the darkness," Mrs. Ethel smiled. "And I think your gas is here."

A truck pulled up with a man bringing four gallons of gas.

"How can I thank you, Mrs. Ethel?"

"Go home and love on that wife of yours. Put some gas back into what matters in your life. Work won't hold your hand when you are dying."

Mike hugged the old woman and said goodbye. "I'm going to come back and visit you often. I promise." Mrs. Ethel smiled and just blew him a kiss.

The next day, Mike and his wife pulled down the gravel driveway. "This is it. This is where she lives."

But as they got to the end of the drive, all that was there was an unoccupied, rundown white house covered with vines.

"I swear, she was here. This is where I got shot. And where I shot two bad guys. I used her phone to call AAA." They got out and walked around the old, abandoned house.

"I don't care, Mike. All I know is that you are a changed man." His wife patted his back like he was completely nuts.

Then, as she did, she noticed something bizarre on his jacket sleeve.

There was a bullet hole.

She looked at her husband and just hugged him. Apparently more than a bullet wound had been healed last night.

As they got back into the car and headed south, a familiar song played on the radio.

"And praise will come to those whose kindness
leaves you without debt
And bends the shape of things
that haven't happened yet."

The Last Joke

This weekend, I saw my dad take three things, combine them and make a very funny joke. While dementia is stealing his memory, he still has his sense of humor. He's still there. He still remembers me. He is still proud of my boys. He spends his days standing by the fire and greeting people when they walk in the memory-care home. And he beams when I walk through the door.

When he says he loves me, I know he means it. Through all the mourning and pain, that's a balm that heals.

I know that his light will eventually flicker out. And I dread that day. I've had a taste of it already. Last November, he didn't know he had a son. That hurt. I've had some other remarkably painful moments for other reasons — some that just don't make sense. So many of you have gone through this. You understand. Dementia is the devil walking the Earth.

I'm roadweary. And I'm sad. I'm frustrated and disappointed. But honestly, this has made me realize how special my wife and sons are to me. They are positive souls that have kept me sane. I realize that while I can't change people or events, I can make sure I never go down certain paths. I can be a great father and husband. And a good brother to my sisters. I hope my parents realize what special daughters they have. I know I do.

My dad lost his two first-cousins to dementia and I know this is a nightmare for him. I get that. Because it's now my nightmare that I can't seem to wake up from either. Losing him this way sucks. Sorry – there isn't a better way to put it.

All I can do is love and do what I can. I'll be grateful. And I'll dread the day when I hear my last joke from my dad.

SEND IN YOUR PLEDGE OR ANOTHER DOWNTON ABBEY CHARACTER DIES.!!
SCRIPT
THE MOST SUCCESSFUL PBS PLEDGE DRIVE EVER.
MARSHALL RAMSEY

Heat Lightning

On an old porch, a small boy sat with his mother. Lightning flickered on the horizon off toward the Yazoo River. The boy, frightened, asked his mother if they'd be safe from the storm.

"It's just heat lightning," she said. Her hand shook as she spoke.

It was the first of many lies she would tell him. A storm was coming — and not just one from the sky. He was six and soon she was gone. His grandmother, a stern woman with short gray hair and a shorter temper, would raise him. He never saw his mother again.

Thirty years later...

Lightning flickered across the sky. Watching the clouds, he thought of his mother and wondered what had become of her. He had wondered off and on about her for 30 years — mainly when there were incoming storms. "It's just heat lightning," he thought to himself. "Just heat lightning."

No.

The air was thick. Humidity choked the Mississippi Delta — so thick that even the mosquitoes were swimming. He sat on the tailgate of his pickup truck. Lightning flashed again, illuminating the towering thunderhead. Next to him was a small boy.

"Dad, is that heat lightning?"

He looked down at his six-year-old son and said all he could say, "No. It's an incoming storm. But I'll be here to protect you. And I'll always be here for you."

CW's Story

Today, I met CW. CW is that guy you normally walk past. He's on the cleaning crew at *The Clarion-Ledger* and usually quietly goes about doing his job. This particular morning, I was in the vending area and saw him emptying the trash. Maybe it is because I used to be a custodian, but I have a habit of talking to people who clean. And this morning, I am glad I did. Let me tell you a little about CW. He will be 65 soon and is looking forward to retiring. He gets up at 3 a.m. and then as soon as this job is done, he goes and roofs houses. After that, he works three hours at a local University. Like Valerie, he works long hours to get by. He asked me about what I did and I told him. I told about what I do at *The Clarion-Ledger* and what I do on my other jobs. He smiled and said he had admired my work he had seen on my desk. I smiled and said I admired his work as well.

And I do. Very much so.

I had a grandfather who had an insane work ethic. A bit of it has been passed down to me (although I still claim I am a lazy man hiding in work clothes). I think because of my grandfather, I admire people who bust their butts doing the job. I think it's because I want to be like them when I grow up. If I ever do.

I look forward to getting to know CW better. Just meeting him has inspired me to work a little harder, to smile a little more and to appreciate my job even more.

The Canteen

1973

A little boy ran across the field to hug his grandfather. The older man was tall, wrinkled from years of sun damage and slightly hunched. The boy, towheaded and freckled, ran full speed into the man, causing him to drop an old, aluminum canteen.

"Why do you always carry that canteen, grandpa?"

The 50-year-old man smiled and hugged the little boy and said, "You never know when you might need a drink."

The little boy, whose name was Joey, was puzzled. "There's a hose by the barn."

The grandfather smiled and patted his grandson on the head. "You're right, Joey. Now, let's go home and see what your grandma has whipped us up for dinner."

Joey lived with Joseph and Hilda Ryan on a small farm in the northern Mississippi hills. His mother had died when he was born and his father had died soon after while serving in Vietnam. When most people were thinking of retirement, the couple faced the challenge of raising a second son. Through waves of grief, they saw the beautiful face of a child who needed their love. Joseph Ryan stood stoically at his son's funeral. A single tear trickled down his weathered face.

1979

The preteen watched his grandfather in church. He noted the way the older man carefully prayed and sang at the top of his lungs. He worshiped with the zest of a man who knew God personally. Joey listened carefully to his grandfather stress "forgive my trespasses as I forgive those who trespass against me." Joey also noted the canteen sitting next to his grandfather. "Why?" he'd ask. And his grandfather would never really tell him why.

1986

"But I want a Honda Accord!" Joey protested yet got nowhere with his grandfather. His grandfather was a loving, tolerant man. But he would not bend when it came to Japanese cars. Joey didn't mind, though. He loved his Chevrolet Camaro. He and his grandfather would ride around with the T-tops out. And next to his grandfather was the old man's canteen.

1988

The cake read, "Happy retirement!" His grandfather had farmed in the morning and delivered mail the rest of the day. Known in the small town of Corinth as "Mr. Joe," he was a beloved fixture in the fabric of the community. Joey came up from Ole Miss for the party. He hugged his grandfather and gave him a special gift: Two tickets to the Egg Bowl. It was one the finest days of Joseph Ryan's life.

1991

The grandfather was Joey's best man. "Mom and Dad would have really wanted to see me get married," he said.

His grandfather took a swig out of his canteen and said,"They're here. Trust me, they are here."

When his grandfather wasn't looking, Joey picked up the canteen and sniffed it. "I bet the old man drinks." But it wasn't booze. It was just plain water.

1996

At the Baptism of the Joseph Ryan IV, Joey heard his grandfather praying for forgiveness again. "Grandpa, do you ever worry about going to hell?"

His grandfather paused and rubbed his chin. "No, Joey; I've been there." He picked up his canteen and left it at that.

2013

Joseph Ryan lay dying in his hospital room. Melanoma cancer had ravaged his body – a curse from years of intense sun damage. He called his grandson closer and hugged the man. "It has been my greatest joy raising you. Your father would be so proud of you. I know your grandmother and I are." His breathing became more labored and alarms began to sound. And as he started to pass on, his grandson looked at his grandfather and asked one last question, "I love you, too, grandpa. But tell me one thing. Why the canteen?"

His grandfather gripped the old aluminum canteen and said one last word, "Peleliu."

The next day, Joey allowed the strange word to rattle around in his head. Peleliu. Where had he heard that word before? Peleliu…what could it mean?

And then it hit him. He remembered it from the miniseries, "The Pacific." It was one of the most hellish battles of World War

II. He went into his grandfather's room and saw a small box by his bed. In it was a globe and anchor — the emblem of the United States Marine Corps. An old photograph of a bunch of Marines on a scarred tropical island. A signed copy of "With the Old Breed at Peleliu and Okinawa" by Eugene Sledge. Joey read the inscription: "To my good friend Killer. It was an honor to go to Hell and back with you."

Joey began to read the book. The battle of Peleliu was one of the fiercest, nastiest battles in the Pacific. Marines invaded a 5-square mile island what was supposed to take three days to take. It took over 30. The Japanese Army was dug in over 500 caves. The island was one big kill zone. And to make matters worse, it was 115 degrees in the shade. The Marines had no water in the initial phase of the battle. His grandfather's canteen suddenly made sense. He had been to hell. And nearly died of thirst in the process.

At the funeral, Joey and his son stood by the grave as the most important man in their lives was lowered into the ground. Family and friends sprinkled dirt on the coffin as Joey walked up to the hold. He bent down and placed an aluminum canteen on top of the coffin.

"I know you won't need this where you are going, grandpa. But here's an extra one just in case."

And as Spring spread its green blanket across the Mississippi countryside, everyone at the graveside toasted his own aluminum canteen the memory of a real American hero.

Finding Empathy in the Middle of Rush Hour

I was temporarily stuck in traffic this morning and I decided to look around at the people surrounding me. There was a balding man, probably my age, driving an older four-door sedan. He had a worried look on his face — I began to make up a life for him (I do that a lot). He probably had a family. Or he could be going through a divorce. He might be worried about his job. Or he could just have to pee because he drank too much coffee. On the other side of me was a younger woman, probably 25 or so. She had a small SUV and was busy tapping on her phone. I could see her smile — whatever it was she was reading brought her a moment of joy.

We pass strangers every day and just let them pass us by. I thought about that as I watched the people in the cars. Every one of those people has a story. Every one of those people has something he or she is dealing with. It may be a tragedy. A divorce. Sickness. A loss of a job. Drugs may be destroying someone in the family. They may be battling the bottle themselves.

It's easy to get caught up in your own drama or even some trumped-up controversy on cable news. Lord knows I have gotten worked up over my own stuff recently. But at that moment, when I was sitting in traffic, I thought about my purpose on this Earth. And I thought, if I can bring a moment of joy to someone else — someone who is going through their own hell, then maybe a good life is possible after all.

Empathy is hard to find when you're caught in rush hour traffic. But for a brief moment, I felt it.

SO CLOSE AND YET SO FAR...
HOUDINI'S SECRETS
PIP
MARSHALL RAMSEY

Son of a Beach

Gray clouds hang over the brown Mississippi Sound, selfishly hiding sunken treasures never to be found.

Occasionally the murky water gives up a prize: A button, a washer or some other surprise.

The killer ocean swept away his life during its prime; now she gave it back, one piece at a time.

A gull squawked at the lone man standing on the Biloxi Beach. He was tall, thin, slightly balding and holding a leather journal. He finished writing and carefully put it in a pocket in his apron. It was time to go to work. He crossed Highway 90 and entered the greasy waffle restaurant.

"Table four needs to be bused. Pronto."

"Good morning to you, too, Donna Ray." Gary Drucker punched the timeclock and picked up his plastic tub.

Biloxi's Waffle Barn No. 3 sprang from the sand like a waterlogged phoenix after Katrina. Gary had once joked that the storm was the first time the restaurant's floor had been cleaned. People didn't joke about Katrina much. But Gary did. He had earned the right the hard way.

"Hurry up, boy. We done got customers waiting."

Donna Ray's shrill voice was like cat claws on a chalk board. She was the cashier/hostess/manager/pain-in-the-butt extraordinaire of Waffle Barn #3. And while she claimed to be from somewhere up North, Gary was convinced she had flown in straight from Hades. Donna Ray was a large woman who smelled vaguely like cats. And she was grumpy. Very grumpy. She was just a big bag of chuckles.

"Yes, ma'am."

Gary was 45 and a busboy. Not exactly how he had planned his life to turn out. He looked back across Highway 90 out at the Mississippi Sound. The sea had taken everything from him, including his sanity. So now he worked odd jobs up and down the Mississippi Gulf Coast until it washed ashore.

He looked at the change on the table. He saw all the presidents he wanted to see — but only on coins and not paper. Waffle Barn wasn't the place to get rich. In the distance, he could see the fool's gold known as Seaside Casino. Maybe someday he could get a job waiting tables at Johnny Steak's House of Meat.

He'd be rolling in the big bucks. If only he could work at the House of Meat.

House of Meat. Who the hell named a restaurant "House of Meat?" It really sounded like dirty in a 6th grade joke. As opposed to the wholesomeness of "Waffle Barn." "Excuse me ma'am, would you like to join me and eat at the House of Meat?"

Gary laughed at his own joke.

Waffle Barns had popped back up after Katrina like mushrooms. There was a small fortune to be made in feeding relief workers who had descended on the coast like helpful locusts. But now the rebuilding had stalled and the workers had gone away. Quaint middle-class residents had gone the way of barge-based casinos. The insurance was too high for anyone to rebuild – unless you could afford a disposable house. Gary couldn't do that. His family's home had washed up down the beach. His wife nearby. Waffle Barn No. 3 wasn't far from where he found her. It's why he couldn't leave.

Waffle Barn No. 3 was his purgatory. Gary had sins to be forgiven.

He plopped the dirty dishes into the bucket. They never should have stayed. "The house survived Camille," he remembered telling his wife Judy. He could hear his words every night in his nightmares. The house HAD survived Camille. But Katrina wasn't Camille. He also had nightmares of the surge crashing through the front windows. And of the house collapsing while they were in the attic. He heard her screams for help. He saw Judy's blue face. He had killed her.

Gary's eyes burned. Must have gotten something in them. Or something.

"Hurry up over there. You got molasses in your veins?"

Gary wanted to tell Jabba's twin sister to shut up. But just he smiled and said, "Yes, ma'am." Being polite was a Southern thing. Being polite meant he got to keep this job.

Off in the distance, a small Cessna tugged a banner for Crazy Carl's Souvenir Emporium. Crazy Carl and his Emporium were institutions along the Gulf Coast. It was an empire of imported Chinese knickknacks built on a foundation of family booze money. Carl's daddy had bootlegged and gambled during the Coast's wild years. Before Camille. Carl took the trust fund left to him and invested it in tacky souvenirs.

Carl was also Gary's older brother. The two didn't talk much. After 45 years, they had just run out of things to say. The last thing Carl had said to him was, "You killed her, you know." Carl still was missing his two front teeth.

"You ought to ask your brother for a job." Donna Ray noticed the plane's banner and threw her unwanted opinion in. It lay on the floor, stinking like a dog turd.

Gary shivered at the thought. He'd rather swallow more sea water than his pride.

At table #5 sat a blond that looked vaguely familiar.

"Gina?" Gary said with a smile. "What are you doing home? And how are you doing? I lost track of you after you got laid off."

Gina was a reporter for *The New York Times*. She had profiled Gary when she was a reporter for the local paper *The Sun Herald*.

"Gary, is that you? Her voice sounded genuinely excited. "I'm here to do a piece on the Katrina anniversary. I took a job in Memphis and then the *Times* hired me. I'm surviving. You know how the newspaper business is these days. You live day to day."

Gary understood. He had been doing that since the storm.

"I want to show you something," Gary blurted out. Living alone meant he didn't talk to many people — only his cat Gulfport. And Gulfport wasn't much of a conversationalist." Gary reached into his apron pocket and pulled out a black leather notebook.

Gina took the book and said, "What's this?"

Gary said, "Open it and read."

Inside were amazingly descriptive poems and stories based on Gary's daily walks on the beach. It was a eight-year journal on one man's odyssey back from the brink.

"These are amazing. Mind if we publish a few of these? I want to write a story based on your journey. These could really help others who are going through what you're going through. Lord knows many in New York and New Jersey could appreciate your journey. Sandy kicked them in the teeth pretty hard, too."

Gary thought about it for a moment. And then said, "If it helps, sure." It was his moment. He felt at peace.

The New York Times Magazine ran a feature on him and his poems. Soon he was on talk shows and reading his poems in New York — When Donna Ray would give him the time off.

Random House published a compilation of them that was illustrated by famous water colorist Wyatt Waters. *Son of a Beach: Tales From the Eye of the Storm* quickly became a *New York Times* Best Seller. He charmed *The Tonight Show's* Jimmy Fallon and the rest of the country. Critics said his writing was funny, brutal and honest. There was something about his candor. He had stared the Devil in the face and the Devil had blinked. People needed to hear his story. Gary soon had enough money to quit Waffle Barn No. 3.

But he didn't.

He continued to bus tables. He stayed in Purgatory by choice. He decided to stay there to help others out of it.

He spent all his free time writing and working as a counselor at the local hospital. And petting Gulfport and heckling Donna Ray. It was a good life. A simple one. He grew where he was planted.

One day as he was walking down the beach, he noticed something glimmer. He bent over, brushed the sand away. It was Judy's locket. The ocean had returned a hostage. The ocean sent back his sanity.

Gary had paid for his sin. Now he was busy helping others recover from theirs.

The killer ocean swept away his life during its prime; now she gave it back, one piece at a time.

Why We Train

It's Friday. Your bed is warm and the floor is cold. You muster the energy to get your feet on the ground and head to the gym – but you're sore. Tired. Worn out. Your muscles burn. You don't want to be there. You could just go through motions. You know, give half effort. I mean, who would know if you did? It's a victimless crime, right? Just coast on through the workout to the weekend and everything will be just fine.

But you don't. You reach down inside of you and pull out a little more effort. You lean into your exercises and get the most out of them. You hurt. You're tired. But your body responds when your brain tells you it can't. You unmask your brain for what is: A liar. You push. Sweat drips down your face and into your eyes. The sting reminds you that you are alive. And when the hour is up, you feel a sense of satisfaction that powers you through the day. You wanted this. You trained your muscles.

And you trained much more.

It's Friday. Your bed is warm and the floor is cold. You muster the energy to get your feet on the ground and go look for a job – but you're sore. Tired. Worn out. Your heart aches. You don't want to move. You could go through the motions. You know, give half effort. I mean, who would know? It's a victimless crime, right? Just coast through your life and everything will be fine.

No, it won't be fine. You have people depending on you. So you reach down inside of you and pull out a little more effort. You lean into your life and get the most out of it. You hurt. You're tired. But your body responds when your brain tells you it can't. You continue to push. The sting of fear reminds you that you are alive. You feel a sense of satisfaction that powers you through the day. You needed this.

You've trained much more when you worked out.

You trained your will.

The Drink

Life had kicked Kyle Dryer hard and now he was trying to prop himself up with a bottle.

"Here's to being a complete screw-up!" he drunkenly toasted the sky. The empty bar did not toast him back. Kyle Dryer was losing and was acting like it.

"My job is a joke. My wife is cold. My kids are screwed up. Thanks, God for nothing."

Ed the bartender wiped out a glass and stacked it on the bar. He had heard this speech many times before. It seemed that every pity party keynote speech blamed God.

Kyle yelled, "Give me another, bartender. And make it snappy."

The bartender wondered some days if this was worth it. This was his second job — a job that helped put his special needs child through school. He felt his jaw tighten as he poured another drink. He felt like an enabler for fools.

"Here you go, Ace," he slid the glass toward Kyle. "Enjoy."

Kyle threw a fistful of dollars at the man. "No, you enjoy."

"A-hole," the bartender mumbled under his breath. No one enjoyed a pity party except the person throwing it.

But Kyle Dryer wasn't an a-hole. He was a good man who had lost focus. He took another swig and looked up, "Why?"

A voice said, "To make you better, that's why."

Kyle swung around, looking for the source of the voice. He couldn't see it.

"Oh, I'm here. Walk on over to my booth. We need to talk."

Strange — the bartender didn't act like he had heard anything. Kyle picked up his drink and walked over to the corner of the bar. It was dark and particularly smoky. But it didn't smell like cigarette smoke. In fact, it had no smell at all.

Kyle set his drink down and tried to make out a face on the man. Nothing. A hand reached out into the slight beam of light and touched his bourbon. Kyle noticed it turned from gold to clear.

"Now, we can talk. I needed your undivided attention."

Kyle interrupted by asking, "What's your name?"

"I go by many names, son. Names aren't important. Just call me a friend."

Kyle shifted uncomfortably in the booth. The hardwood bench pinched his back. He had a feeling his pity party had just ended.

"Remember when you played basketball in high school and you almost got cut from the team?"

Kyle said, "How do you know that?!?"

The voice continued, "Did you quit? Did you blame God or anyone else for your problems?"

"Um, no." Kyle stuttered," I worked my butt off. I went to the gym early before school and shot free throws until I got blisters. I eventually made All-State and got a college scholarship."

"How's this any different?"

"This isn't a game; that's how it is different." Kyle's voice had a touch of indignation.

"Exactly. It's more important. And yet, you are in here harassing my favorite bartender instead of doing what you need to do to make things better."

"But this is overwhelming. I don't know why so many bad things are happening at once. You're so smart — tell me why."

"Because like when you played basketball, I know you have greatness in your heart — that's why. You must rise to the challenge. Diamonds are just coal with heat and pressure."

Kyle looked into the darkness and saw his father's face. And then his coach's. And then his mentor's. He then saw the face of his wife, his child and his boss.

"Yes, Kyle. We all are there to make you better. You can change the world. You just have to believe. And then do. Now go, son. Get busy. People need you. The hard times are what polish you. They make you great."

Kyle picked up his bourbon and took a swig.

It was water.

So Here Are a Few Tips for Coping with Driving on Today's Sleet and Ice.

• Get the flu. Staying home is your best option.

• Act like you have the flu. Even better. That way you won't have the flu.

• Get your teaching degree. You stand a better chance of staying home when there is ice. Administrators try to avoid having buses full of children plunge off of icy bridges.

• When you get to a bridge, slam on the brakes. Seriously, don't do that. But it seems like most of you do. Ease off the gas and coast across the bridge instead.

• Black Ice is not an illegal drug made in a RV by a guy named Walter White. If the road looks wet and the temperature is below 32, it's safe to say the road is icy.

• Elevated surfaces freeze first. That includes bridges, overpasses, culverts and politicians' egos.

• Scrape your windshield — unless you like driving blind. Apparently some of you do.

• Pray. Because it seems like most of the cars around you have decided to let Jesus take the wheel.

• Wait and let others do the wrecking for you. If you can telecommute, great. If not, let the trailblazers get out there and play demolition derby for you.

• Have a buddy with a 4×4 truck and a chain on speed dial.

Godspeed folks. And remember. When in doubt, slam on your brakes. Life is too short. Make it shorter.

ONCE JIMMY HOFFA IS FOUND, WE CAN MOVE ON to FINDING JIMMY BUFFETT'S LOST SHAKER OF SALT.
FBI
FBI
MISSING
MARSHALL RAMSEY

IceFreakOut 2015 Coverage

Welcome to special IceFreakout 2015 Coverage, I'm Cordon Bleu.

And I'm Melanie Marsha Maggie Megan.

Tonight's top story is the psychotic weather. We now go to our Chief Top Grand PooBah Meteorologist, Storm Front, who is in our Weather Lab — which is three feet away from me.

Thanks Cordon. Tonight's weather conditions are sponsored by Lithium. Well, it's colder than Elsa's armpit out there tonight, folks. This after a high today of 84 degrees. Yep, if you don't like Mississippi weather, wait around for the next commercial break."

Storm chuckles at his own joke and continues.

"We've turned on our high-powered Mississippi Electric Super Duty Doppler Microwave 3-D Radar Range Radar and you can see the frozen precip headed down I-55. I'll be back with the five-day forecast after some news and lots of commercials. The forecast is sponsored by bread and milk. Break and Milk, just add eggs and you have French Toast.

Cordon speaks: "We're going to skip the usual murder and mayhem to go straight to our reporter in the field, Ima Freezin."

A young reporter shivers while standing in the middle of the interstate.

"Cordon, the windchill is dropping faster than my core body temperature. In fact, I can't feel my face. My lips are blue. My cameraman's eye is stuck to his camera. If you'll notice, the weather is now causing a huge backup on I-55."

Cars honk and drivers shout obscenities. A 1996 Malibu slams into the back of the live truck, which is parked in the center lane of the Waterworks Curve.

Melanie Marsha Maggie Megan comes on after the screen goes blank. "We seem to have lost the signal. Right now, we have the following school closing updates.

"Clinton, Rankin, Madison and Jackson Public Schools might be closed. Maybe. They'd tell you but they'd have to kill you. Parents are advised to panic now.

"And we have this just in from Gov. Phil Bryant. State employees are to report to work at 10 a.m., unless he cancels work all together at 9:59 a.m. Stay tuned and get ready to be stuck in your car."

Cordon interrupts Melanie Marsha Maggie Megan: "We have Ima Freezin back."

"I'm OK, Cordon. Apparently, parking the live truck in the middle of the Waterworks Curve was not a good idea. I can now report that I-55 will be closed for the next 12 hours."

"OK, Ima, thanks for that MDOT Traffic Cam update. Now back to Storm Front in the Weather Lab that is three feet away from me.

"There is ice in my sweet tea. And there is a chance it will get on the overpasses and trees. This update is brought to you by Lipton Iced Tea."

Melanie Marsha Maggie Megan speaks, "Thanks Storm. Now for sports. Here is the captain of our sports team, Right-Field Ronnie."

"Big news on the home front. There will be a luge race tonight on the Stack and there will be professional shopping cart races in the milk and bread aisles in Kroger. Otherwise, there are no other sports. Everything was canceled."

Cordon: "Thanks, Right Field. Mother Nature has been arrested on the 500 block of Northside Drive. JPD has charged her with assault and battery. She was led to the patrol car screaming, 'IT'S FREEZING TODAY. IT WILL BE 70 BY THE WEEKEND!!!!!'"

Melanie Marsha Maggie Megan: "One last word on the weather, with Storm Front."

"We're all going to die."

"Thank you and that concludes our special coverage of IceFreakout 2015."

The sound goes down as the anchors idly chitchat.

Editor's Note: None of my hardworking TV friends were harmed in the making of this blog.

The Painter

I was sitting in the University of Tennessee's Circle Park, reading a book on metaphors and pondering what I'd do with my life. College was almost over, real life loomed ahead of me and I had no clue what was next. The future should have been exciting. Instead, it scared the Hell out of me.

Spring meant that the azaleas and the dogwood trees competed for the eye's attention. Nearby, an older man patiently dabbed his brush onto a canvas. He was meticulously recreating the scene — yet in a way, what he saw was more beautiful. The colors were more vivid. The scene was more intense.

My book became less interesting as I continued to watch him paint. How could black and white words compete with such glory? I stood up, dusted myself off, walked over to him and sat down on the ground.

And then I just watched.

He was oblivious to his audience — or at least seemed to be. After about 30 minutes, he acknowledged me with: "Spectacular, isn't it?"

I wasn't sure if he was talking about the scene or his painting. I answered, "Um, yes. I hope you don't mind if I watch you paint."

He smiled and said, "If I did, I would have said something by now."

I smiled back. It wasn't the first truth he'd tell that day.

"You paint?" he asked. I didn't at the time (although I do now).

"No sir." My Southern training shined.

"Life's like this painting, you know," he continued.

"Do tell," I sarcastically thought to myself. But I just muttered, "Uh huh."

"We're given a palette and a blank canvas. Some people have more colors. Some people have more skill at applying the paint. But we all are given the opportunity to create a masterpiece. You can mix the paint together with caring and wisdom and create new colors. Or you can slop it together and make mud. It's your choice."

He paused and painted some more.

Then he continued, "But the truly great learn how to see things. And then they make it better. They work hard and continuously add brushstrokes. When the oils permeate the canvas, you've left your mark. Your painting is your legacy. It's the art you leave behind.

I was 23 years old and I had no freaking clue what he was talking about. I wish I had had more wisdom. I wish I had been clairvoyant enough to ask him questions. But I wasn't. I watched him for a few minutes and then walked away.

His wisdom was lost on me — until today.

I walked past the bright flowers of the Governor's mansion at lunch and thought of the painter. I thought about what's on my canvas and what kind of painting I'd leave behind. And then I smiled.

Twenty-four years ago, a painter left a brushstroke on my canvas. And it was pure genius.

St. John's Miracle

Leaking rain dripped onto the young priest's head.

Father Thomas looked up at the Christus Rex and quietly asked, "Why?"

The Christus Rex looked down at him and didn't say a word. It never did.

"Of course, you won't answer. You never do."

Father Thomas was doubting. A man of faith was losing his. He continued to do his priestly duties.

It was a cold, gray, dreary Sunday. The pews were nearly as empty as the collection plate.

St. John's Episcopal Church was dying. And Father Thomas couldn't save it.

Water continued to drip in from the cracked slate roof. Drip, drip, drip, the water hit the top of the Christus Rex. Like water torture, the church had slowly dwindled one person at a time. People died. People moved. Once a bustling congregation, St. John's membership dwindled as the neighbors shifted to the suburbs.

Fresh out of seminary, Thomas Dunn had landed the job at St. Johns three years ago. The Bishop, a short, gregarious man, saw something in the young man. "I normally don't like head rectors to be as young as you are. But you have been touched by God."

Touched by God? What was that supposed to mean? Maybe he meant cursed.

Father Thomas struggled to bring the ailing church back to life. He opened the doors to the neighborhood. He worked repairing houses. He created a preschool for working mothers. Faith became a verb, not a noun.

Still, nothing. Father Thomas felt like he was just throwing matches on wet wood.

He held the wafer in the air and broke it in half. "Body of Christ, bread of heaven."

Rain began to fall harder outside. Water dripped onto the Christus Rex even faster. And then something miraculous happened.

Thomas didn't notice it at first. But soon, there was an audible gasp as blood red streaks streamed down the wall. Father

Thomas turned around and walked to the wall. He stuck his finger out and tasted the red liquid.

"Wine."

"It's a miracle!" screamed Hilda Taylor. Her 75-year-old sister Frieda yelled, "Praise God!" Her 13-year-old granddaughter took a picture of the wine and posted it on Instagram. Before you could say the Lord's Prayer, the photo went viral.

The next Sunday, the sanctuary was full. People came to see the St. John's Miracle. And the miracle energized all areas of church. On Wednesday nights, the Vestry was full. People poured out into the neighborhood to rebuild it. The dying church came back to life. And soon, the community surrounding it did also.

And so did Father Thomas. His homilies took on new energy. He found words that turned words into action.

A year later, Father Thomas turned and looked at the Christus Rex. He smiled and said, "Thanks be to God." Of course, the Christus Rex didn't answer. It never did.

But this time, Father Thomas was a doubting Thomas no more.

Thanks, Dad

I don't remember how old I was, but it was around the time I had my six-year-old molars yanked. My dad and I were in the basement restoring his 1953 Ford pickup. He was up under the hood, working on the engine when his hand slipped, crushing his fingers. What I heard next was a curse word — which was unusual for my dad.

I looked at him and asked, "Isn't it wrong to say that?"

My dad wiped his brow, held his throbbing fingers and said something that has stuck with me for the next 40 years. "I know. But I try to be good to people to make up for it."

That's my dad. Flawed, yet at the end of the day, perfect. A perfect dad for me, that is. And I am sure my two sisters would agree.

His name is Dave Ramsey. No, not that Dave Ramsey, but he is that Dave's uncle and the person he's named after. And please allow me to tell you about him. We have a bad habit of only saying nice things about people when they die. My dad is 79 and is very much alive. I hope he knows I feel this way about him already. But this is what you need to know:

He's ornery, funny, handsome, grumpy, smart, distant yet loving. When he's on his A game, his wit is second to none. He's a master salesman who could sell ice to an eskimo. He loves the Special Dinner at any Mexican restaurant (and will proclaim it to be the best meal he's ever had), UT football, cheap beer, his cats, cars and his children. He and his neighbor owned an automotive garage for years — a place where I saw his generosity first time. He has been physically strong his whole life and waterskied at 78. He beat cancer 16 years ago; it hardly slowed him down. In his career, he sold cars, electronics, chemicals, fasteners and then in 1974, he switched gears and bought a gas station. I admire him for having the courage to change careers like that. Forty years later, I'm doing the same thing.

I can tell you his faults — because I have most of them. He yells when he's frustrated and is stubborn. So am I. Sometimes he doesn't finish a project. Nor do I. And like me, he worked his ass off at his job. He'd work long, long hours — but I always loved seeing his car when he'd come home. He'd always fall asleep in his chair. He still does.

Dad served his country with distinction. He was a corporal in the U.S. Army in the 101st Airborne Division. He also played college basketball and baseball. I sucked at both. I always wondered if that bothered him — that I was different from him. Yet he was proud of me as an athlete and loved watching me play football. Today, he is proud of me now for many other reasons. Once, after I spoke at the Millsaps Arts and Lecture Series, he told me, "You're the only person I've known who knew what he wanted to do when he was eight years old and did it."

It was one of my finest career moments.

A few years ago, I asked him about success. I always wondered if he was totally happy with the career path he took. He told me, "I see you three kids and know I'm the most successful man around."

He had his priorities straight.

When his dad died, I saw him change. He hugged me for the first time at his father's funeral. Losing your dad will do that.

You learn from your parents until they are gone. He's my textbook, good and bad, on being a father to my own boys (who call him Papa Dave). I'm lucky I still have both of my parents teaching me. And I know they both love me. They believed in my crazy dream. He and my mom have left me my inheritance early.

My cousin Dave Ramsey is wildly successful. But I will assert that my dad Dave Ramsey is, too. He has successfully given me a lifetime of memories.

And I just hope I'm as good a dad as he has been to me.

MORE DANGEROUS THAN a BLASTING ZONE...
CAUTION COMFORT ZONE
YOUR DREAMS

Stanley Ryan's Revenge

The first morning rays of Halloween haunted their way through the bedroom's curtains like happy ghosts. Stanley Ryan opened one eye and then another. There was nothing spooky about this morning: He felt great. In fact, he woke up feeling better than he had in years. He knees didn't hurt. Even the scar on his back didn't burn. He looked over to tell his wife of 30 years, Ann. But Ann wasn't there.

"She wouldn't listen anyway." Stanley grumbled to himself. He and Ann were married in name only. He couldn't remember the last time she allowed him to even give her a hug.

But no matter. Even Ann couldn't ruin how good he felt today. He stretched and walked down the hall. There he saw their cat Diablo.

"Hey you little devil" Stanley said to the black cat. But Diablo just arched his back and hissed at him.

"What the Hell?" Stanley grumbled as headed to the kitchen. No stupid cat or grumpy wife would ruin how amazing he felt. He hadn't felt this alive in years.

He entered the kitchen and noticed something strange on the kitchen counter – an empty bottle of pills. He looked at the bottle. Painkillers. And not good painkillers. The kind of painkillers to which he was deathly allergic.

"Did you do it?"

Stanley heard a voice at the front door. It was Ann's doctor, Frank Carbuckle.

"Just like you said."

It was Ann's voice. Stanley rushed into the living room to see Ann embracing her doctor.

"Did you call 911?"

"Yes. They should be here soon."

Stanley saw Ann kiss Frank.

"I've waited for this moment for years…"

"SONOFA…" But Stanley's voice was muted. Almost like he was screaming underwater. Neither Frank or Ann seemed to hear him.

Fear shot through his body. He ran back to his bedroom and looked at his bed. There, lying prone on the top of the covers was his body. The cold truth hit him.

He was dead.

And Ann had killed him.

That night, at Frank's house, Ann and Frank sat at the dinner table in robes.

"I loved the way you cried and screamed when the police came. You should win an Academy Award, dear." Frank raised his glass. "Here's to us and our new lives together."

Ann got an evil smile on her face. After 30 years of living with a loser, she now could be with an accomplished man. A man who knew how to take care of her. A man who listened. "It's just too bad Stanley had to commit 'suicide,' like that."

Both laughed.

Ann got up and gestured toward the bedroom. Her robe opened slightly, in an inviting way.

"I'm going to go freshen up and take a bath. Meet me in the bathroom in 15 minutes."

Frank felt his face flush with anticipation. How that loser Stanley could not appreciate a woman like Ann was beyond him. Idiot. Oh well, his loss. Literally.

Ann walked into the doctor's huge master bathroom. She turned the water on as hot as she could stand and watched as the tub filled to the top. She untied her robe, allowed it to slip to the floor and climbed into the hot water. Steam rose as she felt her old, miserable life wash away.

Then she felt something cold come into the room. The chill gripped her and took the heat out of the bathwater. And then she felt a bitter cold on her shoulders.

Suddenly her head was thrust under the water. She tried to scream and gasp for air at the same time. Her arms flailed but whatever was holding her was just too strong.

And then it released.

She looked up, gasping for breath and swore she saw mist. Then as the mist solidified into shape, she tried to scream…

It was Stanley.

He stared at her and transformed into a fiery demon.

"YOU WILL PAY!!!!" his demonic voice screamed as he grabbed Ann's head and shoved it under the water one last time.

Epilogue:

The anchor tried to look serious as 10 p.m. news. Halloween

night was always full of strange stories. He cleared his throat as the teleprompter began to roll.

"In local news, the widow of a local man was found dead this evening in the home of a local doctor. Frank Carbuckle, an OB-GYN, was charged with first degree murder of Ann Ryan. Ryan's husband Stanley was found earlier today after committing suicide. Police said they received an anonymous tip about the murder. Carbuckle was led from his Bel Air home in handcuffs and is being held without bail."

What I Learned from Being a Janitor

When I graduated in 1991, the job market was almost as grim as it is now – particularly in the media industry. I ended up moving back home, diploma in hand, and working as a high school custodian at Alan C. Pope High School in Marietta, Georgia. My job was to clean six classrooms, the 400-hall boys bathroom and the band room and to scrub the cafeteria. I also vacuumed the library. It was not the job that an honors graduate would seek – particularly one who had won a ton of awards in his chosen field. But it was where I ended up. I was there for my fifth year of high school and I was miserable.

Now I look at it as my master's degree in life. For all the great opportunities I received in college (I would not be here today without them), I also would not be here without what I learned from cleaning tile floors. It was the year that I grew up.

Here are 10 things I learned while being a custodian:

1. Your worst moments can turn into your best. This was reinforced when I had cancer and recently when I had my career turned on its ear. But when I was a janitor (what I thought was the low point in my life), I met a person at the school who had a lovely daughter. That daughter is now the mother of my three children and my wife of 19 years. I wouldn't have met Amy if I had not been at Pope High School. She fell in love with me when I was a janitor. (I think she really married me because she hoped I would clean the house. Oh well.)

2. You are not your job. When people looked down on me because I was cleaning toilets, my pride hated it. But I learned that I am not my job. It's something I remembered when I when I was at the top of my career as a cartoonist. And it is something I remembered when I was made a part-time cartoonist. I've seen too many people crumble when they lose their jobs. My job isn't what defines me. It's what feeds my family.

3. Good people are good people, no matter their social status. Kind of seems like a no-brainer. But I learned that every person has a great story to tell. I worked with great people at Pope, no matter what their paycheck might have been.

4. Never stop learning. Just because I was out of school, I

didn't stop learning. I read library books during breaks. I took classes during the day. That's why I call my year at Pope my fifth year of high school. I read over 50 books that year.

5. A pity party is only enjoyed by the person who is throwing it. I felt REALLY sorry for myself for about six months. Then I realized even I was getting sick of myself. By being miserable, I was creating a self-fulfilling prophecy — I was making my life miserable.

6. Don't be the servant who buries his talent. During my pity party, I had stopped drawing. One Sunday, I went to church and heard the parable of the talents. I realized I was the servant who was afraid and was burying his talents. I started drawing t-shirts, caricatures and cartoons again. My attitude improved and the next thing I knew, one of the teachers had hooked me up with her friend who worked at the local newspaper. The rest is, as they say, history.

7. I learned the value and satisfaction of a hard day's work. Scrubbing tile floors and cleaning bathrooms wasn't exactly my dream job. But I learned that my effort and attitude made the day go by much easier. My work ethic was supercharged back then. It is something I depend on today. And I have appreciated every job I've had since.

8. Stuffing a text book and a roll of toilet paper in a toilet and then pooping on it is not funny. Enough said.

9. Find people who believe in your talent and stick close to them. My friend Luke Prescott, who was a science teacher and the Cross Country coach at Pope, believed in my ability. He gave me chances to draw the CC team's t-shirts. He still motivates me today. There were people who were sent into my life during that year to make sure I became what I am today.

10. Worry won't take you where you want to go. While I was having my pity party, I was completely worried that I'd always be a custodian. I couldn't see the future because I was obsessing with the past. Once I stopped worrying and started taking positive action toward my goals, I started making rapid progress up the career ladder. Within three years, I was a nationally syndicated editorial cartoonist who worked at a national syndicate based in California. It is a lesson that I'm remembering currently as I worry about my future. I know that while times seem tough

now, the harder I work, the sooner great things will happen. It provides hope. And hope destroys all worry.

I like to go over to Pope and run on the track occasionally. It grounds me and reminds me of the year that forged me into what I am today. College made me into iron. Working as a custodian made me into steel.

The Legend of Joe Gulfshores

Everyone is running from something. Some are just better runners than others.

The Dolphin Breeze Resort's pink stucco betrayed its age and the fact that the resort was past its prime. Nestled squarely in the middle of the Redneck Riviera, the Dolphin Breeze catered to working-class families desperately seeking Jimmy Buffett's version of paradise. The sand was white. The water was aqua green. And the beer was cold.

It was mid-July and a warm breeze blew in from the Gulf. Joe Gulfshores (his stage name — even his alcoholic mother wouldn't have named him that), carried his amp and trusty Martin guitar out to the pool. It was a solid gig, one that he had had for nearly 25 years. Joe would set up and play Buffett songs as the guests slowly headed off to paradise. The women got younger and the pay smaller. But Joe hung in there. It beat working.

He tuned his Martin and strummed a few chords. A sunburned lady slathered sunscreen on her rather large belly. A bald man's head reflected the noonday sun. Joe was a master observer. He could tell the guests' lives just by watching them. The conventioneer trying to pick up the daughter of another conventioneer — he noted the white line on his ring finger. Everyone was running from something, Joe thought. Some are just better runners than others.

He began to play Crosby, Stills and Nash's *Southern Cross*. "She's all that I have left, and music is her name." Joe smiled to himself. How true that was.

Bob the Bartender (not to be confused with Bob the Builder) poured another beer and looked out at Joe.

"We've worked with Joe for over 20 years and I don't know a damn thing about him."

The new waitress Jenny looked at the little hut where Joe sang. "I was about to ask you about him."

Carolyn, who had managed the poolside grill since the resort had opened, said, "It's easier to give a cat a pill than to get Joe to talk. He'll ask you a thousand questions but you ask him one and he just shuts down. But still, there's something familiar about him."

Six o'clock rolled around and Joe carefully put his Martin in its case. It was a daily ritual for him. He'd pack up and practically evaporate. No one knew where he lived. No one knew anything about Joe.

But Jenny was determined to find out. She sat in her Mustang in the shadow of the resort's parking garage. She watched Joe pack up his Honda CR-V and turn right onto Beach Highway. She carefully stayed two cars behind him. Seven years as an investigative journalist had taught her to disappear into a crowd.

She was going to find out Joe Gulfshore's secret.

Joe turned right onto Jellyfish Court and drove to the large metal gates. Jenny looked at the huge beach homes. You can't afford a place like this as a beach singer. Could he be who she thought he was?

The next day, Joe parked his SUV and unloaded his case. And once again he started with *Southern Cross*.

"And we never failed to fail, it was the easiest thing to do."

Jenny wanted to tell Bob about what she had seen. But she wasn't quite ready to blow her cover. She still had a mystery to solve. Who was Joe Gulfshores? She carried a burger and fries to a man covered with tattoos and listened to her mystery man sing. This guy was too good for this place. What was he doing here?

She noticed his left arm. The skin was crinkled with the consistency of a pork skin. Burn scars. Joe Gulfshores had been burned. But how?

During his break, Jenny walked past Joe and said, "Joe, I can't help but notice your arm." She could see him tense up.

"It's nothing," he said curtly. His tone said it was something.

"Bob," Jenny said when she returned to the bar, "How did Joe get burned?" Bob looked over at the singer and shrugged.

"Dunno. He won't talk about it. Must cause a lot of pain on the inside."

A middle-aged dad walked over to the hut and requested Joe play a song. The song was *Tropical Breeze*, a song by an up-and-coming singer named Bob Seattle. Joe stopped in the middle of the song he was playing and loudly yelled, "NO, THAT SONG IS CRAP! I'll NEVER PLAY THAT SONG!!!"

Everyone around the pool looked at Joe and wondered what they had just seen.

Jenny knew exactly what had happened.

She pulled out her phone and Googled Bob Seattle. Bob Seattle had just signed a huge record deal with Atlantic Records. He was selling out arenas and was working on his second album. But writer's block had gripped him. Then there was the car crash. Two bodies were burned beyond recognition. One was his wife. The other was Bob Seattle.

Or was it?

She looked at the young man with the bushy hair and cheesy mustache. Then she went to YouTube and listened to Tropical Breeze. It was the final clue she needed.

Jenny approached Joe at the end of the day. "Joe," Jenny said, "Or is it Bob?"

Joe turned around quickly and said, "WHAT DID YOU JUST SAY?"

Jenny went back on her heels and then decided to press forward. "It seems I'm not the only one who has a secret."

"Look, I don't know you and I don't care. But my name is Joe Gulfshores, OK?"

"No, you are Bob Seattle and I am going to prove it."

"And you're a nosy reporter from *Today's Music Magazine*. You're not the only one who knows how to use Google."

Both stood a few inches from each other and stared at each other. People walking by would have thought they were having a lover's quarrel.

"No, Bob, I am more than that. I'm your daughter. You know, the one who was raised by your sister after Mom died and you ran away."

Joe's knees buckled.

"Uh....um."

"Don't worry, Bob, I have plenty to say. Why did you run? Why have you hidden in this flea-bitten resort for so many years?"

"I was scared." Bob Seattle looked at his feet. The truth, in the form of his daughter, had finally caught up with him.

"Who was that in the car?"

"I was in the car. I caught your mom cheating on me and hid in the backseat. I was punching her boyfriend when the car ran off the road. He was burned beyond recognition. People assumed it was me." I stumbled home, burned, and scraped together all the cash I had at the house. I left you my royalties and then disappeared into the night. Your aunt knew I was alive. She's about the only one. She would send me money to live on.

"I've looked for you my whole life."

"And now you've found me. Now what?"

"I hate you."

"You'll have to do better than that."

Both stared at each other. Then Jenny began to cry. She fell into the arms of a man she had only dreamed of meeting. A ghost. A minor legend.

"Can you sing? I always dreamed that someday you would sing."

Jenny could sing. Her voice was quite splendid. But she never wanted to be compared to her father. In fact, no one at her boarding school knew she had a famous father.

"Yes."

"Then I have an idea."

Joe Gulfshores walked back out to the pool and picked up the microphone. "I have one more song to play today. It's a request — from that man over there. It's called *Tropical Breeze*." The stunned middle-aged man who had previously had his head bitten off just nodded.

Joe then continued, "Except, I want my new friend Jenny to sing along with me."

The people around the pool stared at the waitress. Who was she again?

Joe picked up his guitar and played the familiar song. His fingers danced up and down the neck of the guitar. A quarter of a century of running evaporated before everyone's eyes. And as he began the lyrics, a beautiful waitress began to harmonize with him.

Bob Seattle came back to life for one more show. He stopped running and started living. And while he would remain Joe Gulfshores to the rest of the world, he gained a daughter.

It was just another typical summer day at the Dolphin Breeze Resort.

The Seeds for Your Best Moments

I have a theory – Your worst moments are the seeds for your best ones. It's the golden thread that holds things together when the world is falling apart around you. Yet it's more than just wishful thinking. It's a philosophy that keeps you going when you feel like curling up in the fetal position. As Sir Winston Churchill wisely said, "If you're going through Hell, keep going." My theory is what provides the motivation to keep going.

And I know on the surface it sounds horribly naive. I understand that when things suck, they, well, suck. When I had cancer, that sucked. When I was fired, that wasn't much fun either. When my job status was changed, it caused some tears. When I was cleaning poop off of textbooks in a toilet, I wasn't living my dream. Now I have a loved one who is very ill – there is nothing good about it, trust me. Life will punch you in the mouth and leave you dazed – and it hurts.

So I know – I can't control what happens to me. I can, however, control how I react to it. When I had cancer, I helped others avoid getting the kind of cancer I had. When I was fired, I learned from my experience and got a better job. When my job status changed, I seized the opportunities that it brought. When I was a janitor, I met a lady who set me up with her daughter who is now my wife and mother of my children. Those bad moments gave me opportunities to have a better life. I just had to train myself to look for them and not dwell on the negative.

And that, my friend, is easier said than done. It's so easy to fall victim to doom and gloom. Fear is seductive. It's easy. It's also a dead end.

As I sit this morning, I am sad about my loved one. But I know this is out of my control. What is in my control is how I react to it. I can choose to be a good brother, son, husband and father. I can look for opportunities to grow and become stronger for my family. And I will. A ship can hit a rock and sink. Or it can be pushed off in a better direction. It's my choice. I'm choosing a better direction.

So as things get tough, I'll keep reminding myself, "The worst moments become the seeds for the best." And as Churchill said, I'll keep going.

HOW to FIND OUT IF A MARRIAGE WILL LAST...
OUR PREMARITAL COUNSELOR TOLD US TO TAKE DOWN WALLPAPER TOGETHER.
MARSHALL RAMSEY

The Tide – A Love Story

The tide came in.

Gulls played along the blue-green surf. Foam tickled the feet of the little girl playing along the water's edge. She dug with purpose, building a sugar-white sand fort.

"This castle will be where I meet my prince charming," she announced to the curious gull. He cocked his head knowingly as a slight breeze blew in off the Gulf of Mexico.

A voice startled her. "Can I play with you?"

The brown-haired girl looked at the skinny, freckled red-headed boy and laughed. "I don't play with boys. Boys are stinky."

The little boy sniffed his armpit. "I don't stink." He walked away with a frown, looking for his own patch of beach to build his dreams.

Ten years later.

The little girl had grown up into a teenager. She and her two friends walked down the beach, looking for boys to impress with their new bikinis. There, at the water's edge, were two boys playing football. One was a god – blonde, muscular and just beautiful. The other, well, the other was skinny and pale. "Hi beautiful!" the pale boy awkwardly said, "Do I know you from somewhere?" He did. But neither of them remembered that moment 10 years before. The brown-haired girl laughed and began flirting with his friend.

Neither of them noticed that the tide was rising.

Ten years later.

The Pensacola Bar was smoky, loud and crammed full of Naval Aviators and women who wanted to meet them. At the end of the bar was a stunning brown-haired woman who was sitting alone. "Five bucks I get her number," the red-headed lieutenant dared.

"You're on," his buddy laughed. "there's no way a scrawny, pale ghost of a man will ever get her to talk to you. And you don't have five bucks. I stole your wallet five minutes ago."

"OK, then can I borrow five bucks so I can win five bucks?"

Both men laughed as the red-headed lieutenant walked over to the beautiful girl and started talking to her.

Maybe it was the white uniform. Maybe it was the gold wings. But the two of them danced on the beach underneath a full

Gulf of Mexico moon.

The rising tide tickled their toes.

Ten years later.

"Push! Push! Push!" The red-headed commander looked as he held his daughter in his arms. She was beautiful — brown eyes and hair just like her mother. And that moment, the tough Navy man broke down and cried. He was in love for only the second time in his life.

It was high tide.

Ten years later.

Storm clouds painted the horizon a sickly green.

He held her hand as she heard the dreaded three words. "We can do your treatment here," the doctor said clinically. "I'm afraid you'll have to have a double mastectomy. And unfortunately, radiation and chemotherapy. Your lymph nodes are involved."

She soon lost her beautiful brown hair. As they walked on the beach — the only place on the planet that could ease her pain — storm-driven waves crashed on the beach. The surge pounded at their feet and threatened to sweep them away. Sand stung their faces.

"You won't love me anymore. I'm not beautiful!" She began to weep uncontrollably.

He pulled her close and held her tightly. Then put his hand on her chest and said all he could say, "What I love is in there. You are perfect just the way you are."

The winds calmed and the waves dissipated.

They were in the eye of the storm.

Ten years later.

Weak from another round of chemotherapy, she shuffled through the sand. "I can't believe it came back."

"It's OK mom," her daughter held her up on one side while the admiral held her on the other. "We will always hold you up."

"I know, dear."

They eased her into the surf. She felt the warm Gulf water baptize her and wash away her fear. Looking up at the two people she loved the most, she felt her pain leave her.

The tide was going out.

Ten years later.

The retired admiral and his daughter carried the urn to

water's edge. They sprinkled the ashes carefully on the warm Gulf water. "I will come back and see you often. And when I see you again, I hope you'll let me play with you," he said.

It was low tide.

As he and his daughter walked out of the surf toward their condo, the admiral had to smile. There, on the same beach where he had met his wife so many years ago, his red-headed grandson was playing with a brown-headed little girl.

The tide came in again.

V-2 Venison Meat Missile

I don't know if his doe wife left him or if he lost his job at the deer factory, but the buck was obviously suicidal. He stood on the edge of Highway 30, cloaked in darkness and fog. He saw my car's bright lights and contemplated turning out his own. His last deer thoughts passed through his deer brain as he prepared for the ambush.

The buck was determined to become a venison V-2 meat missile and I was his target.

Then he had second thoughts. It might have been my car's mighty deer whistle. It could have been me screaming profanity (first you say it and then you do it) out the open window. Or maybe he wanted to raise his son Bambi after all. The buck turned around and ran back into the woods.

I counted 18 venison V-2 meat missiles on my way home from Ripley, Miss. — which means there were about 100 I didn't see. When I finally made it to Oxford, I went the long way to Batesville and then down I-55. A four-lane allows me a little more time to dodge Dasher, Dancer, Prancer and Vixen. And Comet and Cupid and Donder and Blitzen (seriously, who names their kid Blitzen?)

I didn't even bother going down Highway 7. Highway 7 is the deer gauntlet.

As I drove down the interstate, I came to this conclusion: Deer think God has two bright, shiny eyes and makes a deep rumbling sound like a semi. And they want to get closer to God. That's why they stand on the edge of the road. Well, that and the freshly planted rye grass. Grass tastes better the closer it is to a road.

There are several deer seasons in Mississippi — youth, bow, gun and car. Car is year round. I remember nearly hitting one on Christmas eve. My sons cried all the way home. "YOU NEARLY KILLED RUDOLPH."

Rudolph nearly killed me.

But not last night. Rudolph decided to allow both of us to live another day. And for that, I'm grateful.

O'Reilly's War

"Do you know Jesus?"

"Talked to him every day in Afghanistan and Iraq."

"You have an active prayer life?"

"I prayed for my wife to be happy once. She left me the next day. So I'm afraid to ask God for anything else."

The clean-cut young man looked curiously at the 40-year-old bearded man in the doorway. A three-legged, one-eyed dog hopped past them and tried to hike his leg. He fell over.

"That's Cy. As in Cyclops. Was going to call him Lucky, but that joke has been taken."

The clean-cut young man said, "Um, would you like to hear more about how to have a relationship with God?"

"No thank you. If I didn't have a relationship with God, I wouldn't still be here."

Cy hopped back into the house, barked twice, spun once and fell over. He prepared for a nap.

"Have a good day and God bless, you my bike-riding friend." Sean O'Reilly gently closed the door in the missionary's face. The missionary gave up and left.

"How 'bout that, Cy? He wanted to save my soul. Don't think he's up for that job, though. Even the Pope would struggle fixing mine."

Cy barked at his master. Truth was, he had already saved O'Reilly's soul. A good dog will do that.

O'Reilly sat down on the tattered green couch and felt his prosthetic. He had been riding in the lead Humvee when his SEAL team was hit by an IED. "Dam' Taliban. Dam' Iranians. I sure miss my leg." Cy panted in agreement. He missed his leg, too. Cy had been hit by a car and abandoned on the side of the road. O'Reilly found him and did first aid on the small terrier. He saved the little dog's life. Now the little dog was trying to return the favor.

Coming home from war and adjusting to civilian life had been more of a struggle than war itself. For 20 years, he had been a Navy SEAL. BUD/S training made him tough. Combat made him tougher. Marriage made him the toughest. His high-school sweetheart Vicki had been the love of his life. But he hadn't really been there for their whole marriage. And when he was there, well, it was too much for her to handle. Cy hopped over to the couch and begged to be picked up.

Cy had filled a big hole in O'Reilly's heart. A good dog will do that, too.

O'Reilly felt a storm coming on — the dark times when the post traumatic stress disorder (PTSD) were the worst. He had stuck his pistol in his mouth a couple of times. But SEALS don't quit. And who would feed Cy? So he gave up the booze, put his pistol away and sought help at the VA. If paperwork and red tape only cured PTSD, he would be happier than an astronaut in a Tang factory. O'Reilly couldn't be too mad at the folks at the VA. They had a hard job with lots of customers.

O'Reilly felt like he was fighting this one alone. People just did not care.

That's because most Americans had no idea how many veterans were suffering. And most Americans were oblivious to the fact that there was even a war in Afghanistan. O'Reilly had the same nightmare every night — a small boy shooting at him with an AK-47 assault rifle. O'Reilly would pick up his M-4 and begin to squeeze the trigger. But before he could shoot, the little boy vaporized into a red mist from the cannon of an orbiting AC-130 gunship above.

War was Hell and O'Reilly was on an extended tour of duty. He wore his scars on the inside and out. And as tough as he was — and he was tough — this had been the hardest battle he had ever fought.

So he decided to surrender.

"God, it's me again. Yes, you remember — the one who wanted his wife to be happy? Yeah, you kind of owe me on that one. Look, I kind of have this nightmare thing going on. I really need it taken care of. And thanks for Cy. I know angels come in four-legs now. Or, as in this case, three."

O'Reilly looked at the picture of his old man. His dad had been in Vietnam — and had never said a word about that war. But O'Reilly had heard him crying late at night. His father never had the resources he had. His father's life had been cut short because of it.

O'Reilly was the one who had found his body in the closet. That was a hell of a thing to do to a 16-year-old. He never could forgive his dad. Now he completely understood.

"I'm a warrior. But please allow me to have a little peace."

And with that, O'Reilly and Cy drifted off to sleep. The little boy visited him again, but this time did not have a gun. Instead, he held a bouquet of flowers.

This story is inspired by the heroism and sacrifice of so many Americans since 9/11.

National Center for PTSD — Veterans Administration

woundedwear.org provides free clothing and modifications to wounded warriors and raises national awareness of their sacrifice.

redcirclefoundation.org – helps families of fallen special operators.

Prove Them Wrong

Do you know people who doubt your abilities? Who discourage you? Who don't believe?

Prove them wrong.

Do they make little comments that sting? Are they negative? Have they hurt you in some way?

Prove them wrong.

Take the pain and use it to light a fire in your gut. Use your doubter's disbelief as motivation. Remember their discouragement as you encourage those around you. Be everything they never thought you could be. Take positive action in a negative world.

Success is the best revenge.

Prove them wrong.

I WAS BITTEN BY A RADIOACTIVE SPIDER and BECAME SPIDERMAN.
I WAS BITTEN BY A RADIOACTIVE TICK AND BECAME A POLITICIAN.
VOTE ME!
MILK
MILK
MARSHALL RAMSEY

Mikey's Revenge

Lightning flickered on the horizon. The Mississippi Delta's cacophony of bugs ceased their song.

A storm was coming. And it was going to be a bad one.

The severe thunderstorm's winds, its calling card, kicked leaves and limbs across the levee. Dirt peppered the rental car's windshield as it moved slowly down the inky dark driveway. Mikey Ryan had turned off the Ford's headlights in an effort to be stealthy. Another bolt of lightning illuminated the path ahead of him — but it didn't matter. He knew this driveway all too well. His heart boiled like the clouds above him. It was time to settle a score.

He closed his eyes for a brief second to readjust them to the darkness. When he did, he saw himself as an eight-year-old boy. He could smell the alcohol. He could feel the anger. He felt his self-esteem die. That was the day he vowed never to touch a drop of the devil's drink. From that day forward, he kept himself locked in his room. Books became his guardian. Knowledge became his escape route from this Godforsaken place.

Now, he was back. Like his childhood, paybacks were hell.

Mikey had dreamed of this day. It was what got him through Harvard. Then Yale graduate school. He had changed his name to Michael when he had gotten his MBA. Soon he made more money in one year than this whole damned county. Yes, he thought, this placed was damned. He faced the Devil. But soon, soon he would have his revenge. He wasn't a little boy anymore. He was no longer scared.

He had held this house together though sickness and drunkenness. Recently, an e-mail had been sent to his business e-mail account accusing him of being a bad son. That twit didn't know half the story. No one at the First Baptist Church did. They could act all pious. Jesus knew the truth.

Their perfect household had been a facade. He had soon learned Leave it to Beaver was only a TV show. Mikey knew that if it had been true to life, Ward or June would had been alcoholics and the Beaver would had been emotionally abused.

No dog greeted him on the front porch. He figured his childhood dog was long dead. The screen door banged against the doorframe with the wind. There were no lights on. In fact, the old farmhouse was as dark as his soul.

Mikey almost knocked on the door. He held his hand up to rap on the glass, but then lowered it to the knob. He turned it slowly and opened the door slowly.

He was greeted by the sound of a cocking shotgun.

"I never thought you'd have the courage to come slinkin' back here," a raspy voice emerged from the darkness. "You have some nerve showing back up here after leaving us, you #$%." The profanity slithered across the room like the Garden of Eden's serpent. "I've told everyone how you abandoned me. You are no child of mine."

Mikey's heart boiled with anger. He burned his eyes into the darkness, trying to set his eyes on the source of his pain. It was time for him to end this once and for all. He pulled a pistol from his jacket, aimed it at the voice and...

CRACK!!! BAM!!!

Lightning struck the sycamore tree in the front yard, illuminating the room. There, holding a shotgun, was a shrunken, dried-up, bitter human being. As Mikey felt his anger flow through his hands, the storm's wind blew through the door, scattering papers and blowing the figure into a cloud of dust. The shotgun evaporated, too.

Mikey stood in an empty room.

He put the pistol away and walked outside into the pouring rain. Hail pelted him as he approached two small stones. There were dates on the newest one — 1947–2015. Next to it was another one that read 1948-1993.

He had missed the funeral. Now all he could do was talk to a stone.

"I forgive you," he mumbled. Then he yelled again, "I FORGIVE YOU!!!" And as the last word passed his lips, the wind died, the rain stopped and a storm mysteriously faded into calm.

Northwest Rankin High School Commencement Speech: The Used Dog

I don't write speeches. But I have written what I basically said to Northwest Rankin's graduating seniors last Thursday night. It was a huge honor to get to address them and I wish them a blessed future.

He was a used dog. Not a rescue dog, mind you – you lose that title after your second family. No, Banjo was a high-mileage used dog. He started life in Nashville but was soon relocated to a family in Atlanta. His first family wasn't fond of his digging trenches in their wood floors when he was left home alone. His second family was loving but had another male Border Terrier named Bullet. I don't care who you are, things aren't going to turn out well if you live with someone named Bullet. So we got the call from the breeder from whom we had gotten our other dog.

"I have a free dog for you."

I heard, "I can double your vet bills."

But we drove to Atlanta anyway. There the little brown dog Banjo walked across the room and into our hearts.

(Yes, it is a proven fact that my wife did indeed come through Alabama with a Banjo on her knee.)

When Banjo was 10, our third son was born. Banjo would get up every two hours in the middle of the night with him. We thought, "How sweet; he has empathy."

No, Banjo had diabetes.

I didn't want to show my sons that dogs were disposable. And honestly, he was a big part of our family. So guess who got to give Banjo insulin shots twice a day?

Yup, me. Mr. I Hate Needles.

When Banjo was 14, my family was out of town on vacation. I was stuck at home with Banjo because I couldn't get off work. One evening, I came home and found him half-dead on the kitchen floor. In tears, I rushed him to the emergency vet.

At 3:30 in the morning, they called me to say, "You might want to come say goodbye to Banjo. He won't make it until dawn."

All 6'2" of me lay on the table blubbering next to a silly dog. I raised his little black ear and said, "Buddy, if you beat this, I'll write the check."

And before I could get the last word out of my mouth one of his eyes popped open.

Three days later, he walked out of that vet clinic. And I wrote the biggest check I've ever written.

I tell you this story because Banjo proved something to me: If you have it in here (the heart), you can do anything you want to do. Banjo's spirit lives in me to this day.

When I was eight years old, I knew what I wanted to do when I grew up. My family would sit around the dinner table (remember when we did THAT?) and would talk about the day's events. I used to love the crazy cartoons on the editorial pages. Those drawings lit a dream inside of me. But I had to fail miserably before that dream could come true.

In 1991, I graduated from the University of Tennessee with a wheelbarrow of honors and awards. I knew I was going to move to New York and take on the world. Instead, I moved back home and got a job as a night janitor at Pope High School in Marietta, Georgia. It was my fifth year in high school.

I thought it was the worst moment of my life.

So what did I do? I threw the World's biggest pity party. And you know who enjoys a pity party? Only the person who is throwing it. But mine was so epic that I even had snacks.

I was miserable. And sought company. I walked around school with a Xerox of my diploma on my trash barrel and a cloud over my head.

And I did that for six months.

One weekend, I went to church. I highly recommend it (I go at least twice a year whether I need to or not.) As the priest started his sermon, he started talking about the parable of the talents. You know that story – a master leaves town and entrusts his talents (currency) to his three servants. One gets 10. One gets 5 and one gets one. Two servants worked hard and multiplied their talents. But the one who received one buried his. He was afraid he'd lose it.

At that moment, I realized I was the servant who had buried his talent.

I was afraid. I was wasting my talent.

So the next day, I got busy. I drew the teachers' husbands'

caricatures. I did T-shirts for the Cross Country team (I cleaned the coach's room). I drew on the walls and cleaned the marker off (I was a janitor, after all.) I had a new attitude. And doors began to open.

One teacher said to me, "You have a great attitude (something I hadn't heard in a while) – I had a friend who works at the local paper. How would you like an interview?"

"Ha. Of course not. I'd rather clean this textbook out of the toilet."

Three months later, I was pushing a mouse, not a mop.

Another custodian came up to me one day and asked me a question that would change my life. Her name was Maggie and I thought the world of her. Her husband was a pilot for Eastern Airlines and had lost his job due to a pilot's strike. Maggie, who had never had to work, swallowed her pride and worked at the school to keep her family together. One day she came up to me and asked, "How would you like to go out with my daughter?"

I thought, "Your standards are pretty low for your daughter. It's not like I'm going to be a doctor."

Well, I met that daughter and she had the prettiest blue eyes I've ever seen.

I tell you this story because if I had not had the worst moment of my life, I wouldn't have had the four best moments. I got to see those blue eyes walk down the aisle. And I got to see my three boys born with those same beautiful eyes.

The worst moments turn into your best moments.

The worst moments can have silver linings. But you have to look for them. They get you through the toughest of times. I've had other "worst moments." And when they happen, I know that blessings aren't far behind. I've been fired and I've been made part-time. Each "terrible" moment did something very important: It pushed me out of my comfort zone. There is no more dangerous place than your comfort zone. It's that place where you don't even try. It's where you bury your talents.

You will stumble. You will trip. You will faceplant. But, remember, it's not what happens to you. It's how you respond to it. And how you respond to it is determined by what's in your heart.

I think about Banjo a lot. He's no longer with us, but his

spirit lives on. I hope you've caught a little of it tonight. You're about to go out into the world and do amazing things. You will try new things. You will fail. You will succeed. You will chase your dreams.

As I close, just let me say this. I believe in you. And like your parents, I am proud of you. I dare you to do great things. And I know you will. Have the spirit of Banjo.

Bless you and Godspeed on your amazing journey.

The Spirit

First there was the sound of gravel beneath the tires and then the car's engine stopped. The little boy repositioned himself in the back seat after being thrust forward from the sudden stop. His grandfather, who had his arm atop the blue front bench seat, turned his head and said, "We're here."

"Here" was a place the little boy didn't want to be. No little boy wanted to be "here." He sat up and looked out his window. A sign read, "Peaceful Endings Funeral Home."

Protesting would do no good. The little boy knew his grandfather was a polite man. He loved to pay his last respects to the townspeople. But while his grandfather may have found some pleasure in this trip, it flat creeped the little boy out. A stiff was a stiff.

He walked into the room and smelled all the aftershave and cheap perfume. A short line snaked toward the rosewood coffin in the center of the room. It contained Mr. Woodruff, a bank vice-president. But apparently he wasn't a particularly popular man. "Must be more like Mr. Potter than George Bailey," the little boy thought. He loved *It's A Wonderful Life*, for some strange reason. He hoped to be like George when he grew up.

His grandfather walked up to the coffin and peered in at Mr. Woodruff. The little boy peeked around his grandfather at the waxy, ashen face. The man had had something called "cancer," and honestly looked very different from how the little boy had remembered him at the bank.

The little boy just stared.

Whatever was lying in that box wasn't Mr. Woodruff. It kind of looked like him – the mortician was an artist. But the spirit was gone. The life. That spark that made him human. Now he was no different than a piece of gravel out in the parking lot. What was it that made up that spirit? And where did it go? His grandfather told him heaven. Heaven sounded like a wonderful place to the little boy. And he knew Mr. Woodruff's spirit was glad to rid itself of its cancer-ridden host. Almost like a butterfly must feel when it leaves the cocoon.

They headed back out to the car and the little boy stopped and hugged his grandfather. "I love you grandpa." The old man smiled and said, "I know, buddy. Thank you for coming with me today."

Three months later, the little boy looked into another coffin. This time it was that of his grandfather. The line was long from the respectful townspeople who had loved the man. They wanted to pass along their condolences to the family — and to the little boy. He stood there in his J.C. Penney suit with freshly combed hair and tears in his eyes.

"Where did my grandfather's spirit go?" he thought. But he knew. And he knew that in less than a blink of heaven's eye, he'd see his grandfather again.

And he looked forward to that day. Just as long as he never had to go to another funeral again — even his own.

Stuck in the Mud

If you notice my shoes today, they're muddy. And for good reason.

Why? Let's go back to the beginning.

It was last night about 6:30 and life was punching me hard. Some things I have no control of were taking up all my brain's hard drive and RAM. I was making mental mistakes (gas cap left off, for example) as I hustled to get my son to soccer practice. I had fallen asleep previously during his guitar lesson. I was tired and frazzled.

So naturally, I drove past the soccer field where I normally drop him off. My brain was in some kind of automatic overdrive and was taking me to my workout (which was 13 hours previously.) I turned quickly to the right into the back of the field and cut across the grass — something I had done at least a dozen times.

But what wasn't the case the other 12 times was that the field was now a bog. I felt the car sink and then the tires spun. Whirrrrrrrrrr. Mud flew everywhere.

Groan.

The car (which was blameless) was stuck up to the front axles. And all my plans for the next hour were radically changed.

I sent my son to practice and stepped out myself.

Squish.

It was worse than I thought. I went over to a nearby building where a friend worked. He and I got some wood to help the car get some traction. I've unstuck cars a million times. But it wasn't happening today.

The soccer team came over to give it a push. No dice.

I guess I could have gotten mad. But there was no use — Life had decided I needed a reset. And you can't argue with life.

My fingers began dialing the number for a tow truck.

I guess the good Lord had decided He had thrown enough on my plate, because an angel in a truck pulled up at that moment. His name was Jason — and he was dropping off his son just like I was. Except he had a four-wheel-drive vehicle and off-road tires.

"Let me go home and get some rope."

"Good," I thought, "I'm at the end of mine."

He came back about 20 minutes later and we got the car out of the mud in about a minute.

We talked for a few minutes; I really liked the guy. It's funny how a man with a truck and a few straps can renew your faith in humanity. A bad moment had introduced me to a great guy.

I think a younger version of myself would have panicked. Or gotten mad. Or pitched a fit. While I did have a sense of frustration, I knew things would work out. And they did. Maybe it was because I had visited with a friend with lymphoma earlier in the day and had a better perspective. Or maybe I just knew that staying calm was the best option.

I hosed most of the mud off my car last night but didn't clean my shoes. Why? Because I wanted to be reminded that when we sink in life's mud, it takes friends to pull us out.

MARSHALL RAMSEY
"IT WOULD BE PRETTIER IF IT WASN'T POLLEN."

The Lost Veteran

Two Air Force F-16 jets cut through the crisp November sky. The planes' razor-thin wings were breathlessly close as they roared over the small southern city. Beneath them, thousands in the crowd gasped and then cheered. The planes' afterburners screamed a deafening roar as the jets disappeared over the horizon. The annual Veteran's Day parade kicked off in glorious fashion. A little boy named Sam vigorously waved his American flag. A Humvee drove past followed by Marines marching in Swiss-watch precision. All veterans were being honored.

Sam's father had been a veteran, too. Earlier in the year, Sam had worn his clip-on tie as he watched his daddy lowered into the ground. At eight years old, the boy understood the sacrifices the military made more than most Americans. Several Army soldiers marched past. His father Alex had been an Army captain who died in a part of Afghanistan that Sam couldn't pronounce. It was at that moment that Sam went from being an 8-year-old kid to an old man.

Sam's grandfather looked down at him, thinking how the little boy looked so much like his son, Alex. Alex had been all-everything in school. The local congressman agreed and like his father before him, had entered West Point, the Army's military academy. There he blossomed, graduating in the top third of his class. The grandfather watched the soldiers pass by with precision. He saw their closely cropped hair and their steely gaze. One of them could have been his son. The thumping of helicopter blades woke him from his daydream. A National Guard UH-60 Blackhawk helicopter flew low over the parade route. His heart thumped with the rhythm with the rotors.

A block off the parade route, in the shadows of a cold, dark alley, sat a man far removed from the cheers of the loving crowd. Kenneth Gibson's thick, matted beard hid the scars on his face. The scars on his outside, though, did not compare to the scars on the inside. He had seen too much in combat. He had been covered in the brains and blood of his best friends. The Battle of Hue was his breaking point. After that battle, his friends didn't make it home. And truthfully, all of him didn't either. Post-Tramatic Stress Disorder haunted him since. Alcohol and drugs numbed the flames of hell, but they couldn't extinguish them. He sat alone, feeling the cold brick of the alley's wall. The cheering crowd one block away had no idea he was even there. On this Veteran's Day, he had been forgotten. He reached for the near-empty bottle and felt warmth as the cheap whiskey burned his throat. The light of the morning sky faded quietly into darkness.

When the parade had ended, Sam and his grandfather walked back to their truck. Sam looked up at the city's tall buildings. Never had freedom seemed more glorious. He gripped his small American flag proudly. It was a pride from the knowledge that all veterans were being properly honored. They headed south along the sidewalk and for some reason, Sam turned his head and saw a man lying on the ground. "GRANDPA!" Sam ran into the alley. Horrified, his grandfather ran after him into the darkness.

"SAM! COME BACK HERE!"

Sam came up to the man lying on the concrete and gagged. Kenneth smelled like alcohol, urine and death. The grandfather, a former medic, checked the homeless man's pulse. "He's still alive, but barely." He pulled out his cellphone and dialed 911. Then he began to check the man's coat for any form of identification. There he found a phone number on a yellowed, crumpled piece of paper: 1-630-555-2348.

"Hello?" the female's voice answered in a sing-song fashion.

Hello, my name is Samuel Johnson. I found your number in the pocket of a man who we found in an alley. We've called the ambulance. He's unconscious."

There was nothing but silence on the other end.

Then she said, "I think you found my daddy. We've been looking for him for four years now. We had given up and thought he was dead."

"Where are you, ma'am?"

The lady on the other end noted the grandfather's southern accent.

"Naperville, Illinois. We're near Chicago. Where are you? My father is a Vietnam veteran, by-the-way."

The grandfather paused for a moment. "I am a veteran, too. I'll make sure he's well taken care of. Here's my number. " The grandfather gave the lady his information.

The daughter paused and said calmly, "I'll catch the first flight. Thank you."

Later that evening, Sam and his grandfather walked into the local VA hospital. They checked in with the front desk and headed down the hall. There was the daughter, her husband and two other couples. Kenneth Gibson's family stood around a ghost. Sam and his grandfather stood in the back of the room and looked at the scarred face of the Vietnam veteran.

Five minutes had passed until the daughter noticed that they had company. "May I help you?"

"I'm the man who called. My grandson Sam found your dad."

Her tired face lit up with a smile. "Thank you, Sam." She walked over and gave the boy a crushing hug. "Thank you for bringing my dad back from the dead."

Sam wished someone could do that for his father. He looked into the lady's eyes and then said, "You're welcome ma'am. You're welcome."

And on that cold, clear Veterans' Day, those who had served their country were honored – even a lost veteran who had been completely forgotten.

The Flying Keys

Meridian's Al and Fred Key had a problem. The Great Depression had threatened Meridian's airport and they weren't going to allow it to close.

So they did what they did best: They took to the air. And didn't come back down for 653 hours.

Flying a borrowed Curtis Robin, they constantly fed it gasoline during their nonstop flight. The Robin's name? Ole Miss. The Ole Miss now hangs in the Smithsonian Air & Space Museum on the Washington Mall.

Al and Fred took off on June 4, 1935, and landed 27 days later, breaking the endurance record. In the process, they traveled an estimated 52,320 miles and used more than 6,000 gallons of gas.

To service the engine and refuel it, they built a little walkway out to the engine. And to prevent the fuel from spilling (and catching fire) when they finished refueling the plane, they and A.D. Hunter invented a special valve. That valve, in modified form, is what the KC-135 tankers use to refuel planes today. So it's very appropriate that those very tankers are based at that airfield Al and Fred successfully kept open — Key Field.

I look forward to speaking to my friends at Meridian Regional Airport tomorrow. I'll talk to them about how the worst moments turn into the best. Just like what Al and Fred did so many years ago.

The History of a Southern Snowstorm

The day before the storm:

The local TV voiceover guy opened the weather segment with a booming, "This is Eyewitness weather with meteorologist Sandy Storm sponsored by Oger Supermarkets. Oger, for the best bread and milk."

"Good evening, Southlanders. Hold onto your seats. I have big news for you. It's a four letter word that starts with S…"

The producer whispered to the cameraman, "$#*^?" The cameraman jiggled the HD camera as he laughed.

Sandy continued with her big sleet-eatin' grin on her face, "Yes, you guessed it – it's going to SNOW!!!!!"

And at that moment, the whole Channel 5 viewing area exploded into panic.

Bread and milk were the first to go. Beer and toilet paper weren't far behind. Crazed shoppers ran up and down the aisles of the local Oger grocery store in fear. Kids dreamed of a snow day. Parents shook their fists at the sky.

People absolutely freaked out.

18 Hours before the storm:

Thelma Lou Franchesco pushed Wendy Winehouse trying to get a can of tuna. She hit a display of canned corn, sending it and herself flying into the diaper aisle. Tom Drysdale tripped Frank Watson so he could get to the last loaf of white bread first. Fights began to break out at the local grocery store. "How will my baby eat?" cried one shopper as she fell to her knees crying.

"How are you coping with the chance of snow?" asked Buck Strong to anyone who would pay him any attention. Buck was the longtime anchor/reporter legend at Channel 5 news who was famous for once mixing it up with a governor he caught in the same strip-club he was in. Strong's defense was "You can't just find news sitting in your house. Sometimes you have to go to a strip club to find it." Management didn't fire him, but refused to expense the numerous lap dances.

Shoppers hustled past the legendary reporter and into the store, trying to scoop up the last jars of peanut butter and cans of sardines. "Oh the humanity!" one portly man cried.

12 Hours before the storm:

"Do you think we'll be snowed in for weeks?" viewers tweeted Sandy Storm. Sandy kept her 1,000 twitter followers on top of the latest forecast and explained the latest forecast models. "Dress warm!" she replied.

Panic had hit 11 out of 10.

10 Hours before the storm:

Bubba Franklin, the local auto mechanic, readied his four-wheel drive and chain. He'd pull the people out of the ditches. Sure, all the Yankees could drive on snow. But not when there was an inch of ice under it. "I'm providin' a public service," he told Buck Strong. "For $50."

Sandy Storm broke in during the SEC basketball game and said, "Just to let you know, we're under a winter storm watch. I'll break in to tell you the latest." At this point, the basketball fans had already called the management at the station to complain. Sandy didn't mind. She loved to break into prime-time programing.

Road crews busily readied trucks with salt. Bartenders busily readied margaritas with salt, too.

The city had nearly shut down in preparation for Winter Blitz 2013 (what Eyewitness News 5 had now dubbed The Storm.) Now the mayor was ready to enact his emergency plan. (he loved to plan).

8 Hours before the storm:

The city was ready. The population was ready. Kids dreamed dreams of snow men, snow angels, snow balls, snow forts and snow whatever else you can make out of snow. Schools had been preemptively canceled. "We can't risk running the buses during Winter Blitz 2013," said the local superintendent in charge of making such lofty snow-related decisions. The grocery store manager was busy rolling around in a room full of money as he looked out at his store's bare shelves.

Sandy Storm was on the air, wall-to-wall tracking the snow as it came in on radar.

As the sun went down, people huddled in their homes ready for whatever Mother Nature could throw at them. It was all over but the snowing. "Bring it on!" cried Sandy Storm. Buck Strong had hunkered down at the local strip club.

And just as predicted, the first flakes fell. They were

big, fluffy flakes. They quickly covered elevated surfaces and then dusted the grass. Roads got slushy and the surrounding countryside began to look like a Thomas Kincade painting. It was truly a Southern winter wonderland.

Kids woke up to the beauty of the freshly fallen snow and quickly put on their winter clothes. Winter Blitz 2013 had hit. Sandy Storm broke into the morning show to update her viewers one more time.

And then it happened.

The sun peeked over the oaks and the pines and began to illuminate the fresh blanket of snow.

Within 10 minutes it was slush. By 9 a.m. all the snow was completely gone.

Winter Blitz 2013 had ended nearly as quickly as it had begun. It was yet another exciting Southern snowstorm. And all the people had to show for it were kids at home and a whole bunch of milk and bread.

The Past Five Years

When I look back at the past five years, I honestly believe everything bad that happened was placed in front of my path to make me better.

I've faced challenges that made me question my talent, my abilities, my work ethic, my heart and who I am as a person. In that time, I've succeeded – and also failed miserably.

It has been a time of reflection and anger. I've struggled with forgiveness. I've learned who my true friends are.

I needed the past five years and the challenges they brought. After my cancer, I sought security. Security is a mirage that can be blown away with the flick of a finger. What I should have been focused on is embracing change. There is nothing more dangerous than a comfort zone. That's where I planted my flag. I paid a steep price for it.

Build your house on a foundation of stone.

We live in tough times. But tough times require tough people. I now know that I need to put my family first. My wife needs me. My kids need me. Everything else will fall in place. I also need tough personal standards. Hard work and talent are great. But without focus, you get nowhere. So I'm working hard on strengthening my will -– that's why I get up at 4 a.m. to crush myself in a bootcamp. I'm relighting the pilot light in my heart. It's what drives the perseverance required to truly succeed.

I'm a blessed man and a lucky man because I get to do what I love to do. I have my health and my family loves me. Yes, I have struggles. But we all do. I've found that the best way to overcome them is to help others.

So I reject fear. It has crippled me too long. Today, I'm so grateful for the blessing of tough times. And I've thankful for the past five years.

UM, NO.
FRIEND REQUEST
MR. SQUIRREL
PIP
MARSHALL RAMSEY

The Late Arrival

We interrupt this broadcast to bring you the following news bulletin: Flight 903 has disappeared en route from New York to Paris. All 53 passengers and crew are feared lost.

Lightning danced erratically from cloud top to cloud top. It had been an unusually brutal winter and the spring storms had continued to pummel the land well into June. Another flash flickered toward the Delta, illuminating the airport's runway. A storm was coming. And it would be bad.

Mike Branch looked at his watch — 9:55 p.m. It was about time for him to shut down for the night. The small field didn't have a tower per se, but did have Mike manning the radio and the beacon. It was easy work for him – not many planes came in this time of night. The old airport had been an Army Air Corps training base during the great war. Now it was home to a few Cessnas, a corporate jet and a crop-duster.

Another bolt of lightning. This one was closer. Too close if you asked Mike.

The metal trailer shook with the rumble of thunder. There were at least a hundred other places Mike would rather be than in a trailer during a thunderstorm. At the airport, there were a couple of trailers and three metal hangers left over from the war. The Army had left in 1946. The crop-dusters moved in right after the last T-6 Texan left. Rumble. The gods were obviously angry. Mike nervously looked at his watch. He hoped he could beat the storm.

The NOAA weather radio squawked. Mike looked at the screen — It was a severe thunderstorm warning for Warren and Madison counties in Mississippi. The lightning had taken on a strobe-like quality. The blackness of the night turned into day. This was an electrical storm.

"Ground control, this is Flight 903 declaring an emergency. Number four engine is on fire and we need to land immediately."

Mike blinked and looked at the radio.

"I repeat. This is Flight 903. We have an inflight emergency and need to land immediately."

Mike picked up the microphone and said, "Roger Flight 903. This is KMBO. We are a small field — but have a 5,000-ft. runway. A fire station is next door. I can have them on standby.

Will that do?"

The voice on the other end sounded rattled. "Roger KMBO. Fire is now extinguished. Have had a bumpy flight. Encountered severe turbulence. Was stuck by lightning."

Mike couldn't remember a pilot being so chatty.

"KMBO, coming out of storm now. Light up your field."

Mike flipped back on the runway lights. Lightning illuminated a plane on approach.

But something seemed weird.

First, it was a large plane. Mike had thought it was a regional jet.

Second, it was a prop plane. A prop plane with four engines. A prop plane with four engines and a tri-tail.

Mike had seen one of these before. His father-in-law had flown one in Vietnam.

It was a Lockheed L-1409G Super Constellation — an airliner that had last carried passengers years ago.

"Flight 903, could you identify yourself again."

The pilot said, "This is TWA Flight 903. We are flying from New York to Paris and got into a freak electrical storm. All my instruments were fried and we are off course."

TWA? TWA — Trans World Airways had gone out of business in 2001 when it merged with American Airlines.

"Come again, Flight 903. Did you say TWA?"

"Roger."

Mike thought for a second and then keyed the mic. "This is an official channel. I really don't have time for games."

"And I don't have much more time in the air. I need to land and I need to land now. I have injured passengers and need assistance on the ground."

Mike pulled out his iPhone and Googled TWA 903. What he read made his jaw drop.

Flight 903 had disappeared over the Atlantic in 1955. No trace of the airliner was ever found. Mike knew he was being screwed with.

"Um, I don't know who you are, but the FAA will have your license."

But the roar of three Wright radial engines drowned him out.

A white and red plane roared past the field and turned back into the wind for an approach. It looked like a graceful raptor as it touched down on the runway. The giant plane used every inch of asphalt before taxiing to the hanger.

Mike ran to the hanger and pulled old stairs out. The Army had used them for transport planes that would come into the base 70 years ago.

The engines sputtered to a stop and the door cracked open. Another flicker of lightning was followed by the roar of thunder. A face came out. It was the Captain.

"I am so glad to see you. Didn't think we were going to make it." Mike looked at the engine's burnt cowling.

The Captain then noticed Mike's Corvette parked next the hanger.

"Um, what kind of car is that?"

"A Chevrolet Corvette."

"Um, no. I own a Chevrolet Corvette. A brand-new 1955 Chevrolet Corvette. That isn't a Corvette."

Mike pulled out his phone to call the police.

"WHAT IS THAT?" The pilot almost screamed.

"A phone."

The pilot looked around at the planes. He noticed a small corporate jet sitting 50 yards from his plane.

"I flew a jet in the military. That looks more like a space plane."

The co-pilot and flight engineer stepped out onto the stairs. Rain began to fall as a gust of wind blew the flight engineer's hat off his head.

"What day is this?"

"June 5, 2014."

"Not funny. What day is this?"

"The fifth of June in the year 2014."

The flight crew grew noticeably pale.

"Ralph. This is Mike. We have a situation here. Either it's the best hoax ever or I've just stepped into an episode of the *Twilight Zone*." He turned off his phone and looked back at the plane.

He could see the passengers starting to mull around. For nearly 60 years, these men and women had been in some kind of limbo. Now, they would see their children and grandchildren grown old. BOOM! Thunder rattled the earth. The storm started blowing harder as rain pelted the ghost plane and its passengers. Mike climbed up the stairs to meet relics from the past.

Front page of *The National World News*: Ghost plane lands in Mississippi. All passengers perfectly preserved for over 50 years. Elvis seen in downtown Memphis. Bigfoot found with D.B. Cooper's parachute.

Wisdom of a Son

When my oldest son was 10, I took him with me on a speech as a reward for straight A's. This was during the BP oil spill, and the casino where I was speaking was nearly deserted. Heck, the whole Gulf Coast was nearly deserted.

So we're walking through the barren gaming floor on the way to the convention center. There's one lady on oxygen who's smoking. And man who had apparently died while playing a slot machine. My son looked around and said, "Dad this place smells like cigarettes and despair."

It's one of the best descriptions I've ever heard.

Today after our final PLS workout of the week, he wrote an Instagram post that's also worth sharing:

"Had a great first week of doing Paul Lacoste and waking up at 4 in the morning to work out. I learned throughout this week that what determines the successful from everybody else is not if they're fat or skinny or strong or weak; it's how determined they are to achieve their goals."

He's 14 now. Fourteen. I can only hope to have that kind of wisdom when I grow up.

Life's Lightning

Smoke permeated the Delta sky, turning the deep-blue sky gray. Farmers were burning off the last of the season's copious corn crop. Thanks to ethanol, Prince Corn had recently dethroned King Cotton, making the land around the town of Greenwood look more like Indiana than the Cotton Capitol of the world. In the middle of one of those fields, a grand white Victorian home sat beneath five massive oak trees. Two older ladies drank their afternoon drink and watched a gray, striped cat play erratically in the front yard.

The tattered-looking tabby suddenly ran head-first into one of the oak trees, temporarily knocking him out. The two ladies watched. One in horror. The other just shook her head and said, "Percy ain't been the same since lightning struck that tree he was under."

The cat shook his head twice, got up and ran into the tree again. He finally made it past the tree and ran into the bushes.

"Just dumb as a sack of hammers. But any cat that can survive getting hit by lightning has my respect."

Thelma Lynn Jones related to her old cat Percy. She, too had been struck by life's lightning. She had been attacked while on a date when she was 20. She had been in a car wreck in her 30s that killed her husband. She had survived breast cancer when she was 45. Her oldest child had died in the Gulf War. Thelma Lynn Jones's life hit its own oaks trees and she kept going.

A crop duster lazily flew across the smoky sky, spraying a lone cotton field.

"Isn't that Angie? I thought it had crashed." Frances Smith had known the pilot with the plane named Angie. He had recently crashed his crop duster near Indianola.

"Yeah, he's back flying again with a new plane — the Angie II. Tough old bird. Told me a plane crash couldn't keep him out of the air."

"He's crazy."

"Yes. Been that way since he lost his wife. Guess life's lightning struck him, too."

Life's lightning. Those instantaneous flashes when life changes in a dramatic and sometimes tragic way.

A man on a bicycle rolled down the gravel driveway. The

cat bolted out in front of him, causing him to swerve and tumble into the grass. The cat, unscathed, ran back into the bushes.

Thelma Lynn called out to the missionary. "You OK mister?"

The young man, dressed in a shirt and tie, dusted off his pants and his pride.

"Good afternoon, ladies. Have you got a few minutes to talk about the Lord."

"Depends. Would you like a drink?"

The missionary looked at the bottle on the table and said, "No thank you, ma'am, I don't drink. I just would like to ask you ladies a simple question: 'Do you know Jesus?'"

Thelma Lynn pointed to Frances and said, "She went to high school with him."

If looks could kill, Frances Smith would be picking crops at Parchman.

The young man awkwardly laughed, not knowing if it was OK to laugh at such a joke.

"No, ma'am, do you have a personal relationship with our Lord and Savior Jesus Christ?"

Thelma Lynn walked down to the missionary and put her arm around him. They walked together up to the porch. "Young man, I know Jesus. I know God. I talk to both of them every night when I wake up from my nightmares. I cry out for their help when the Devil comes to attack me again. I ask them to lift me up when I see my husband's bloody and smashed face as it stuck through the windshield. I plead for Their mercy when my own cells try to kill me. I fall to my knees as I watch my son lowered into the ground every night. Yes, son, I have a personal relationship with our Lord and Savior Jesus Christ. If I didn't I'd be crazier than that cat."

The cat ran out of the bushes and back into the tree, knocking himself out yet again.

The missionary sat and watched as the crop duster danced across the field. Its yellow paint stood defiantly against the gray sky.

"Like a smooth stone in a stream, my faith is strong, beautiful and a product of my turbulent life. But you want to know something? I wouldn't have it any other way. The worst times in your life are the seeds for your best moments. I'm sure you can't tell me anything I haven't learned the hard way. It's about Grace. It's about forgiveness."

Frances looked at her friend and said, "Forgiveness?!? I can't believe you just said I went to high school with Jesus. If I went to school with Jesus, YOU went to school with Moses."

The missionary looked at the two ladies and asked, "Mind if I join you? I want to hear more about your lives. "

"Want that drink now? We have some lemonade."

The missionary nodded with a smile.

And on that warm fall Delta day, a crazy cat jumped into a missionary's lap and fell peacefully to sleep.

The Courage To Move

Recently, I watched a documentary about the worst aviation disaster ever and it gave me something to think about: Why did some people survive while the passenger next to them perished? And how can I keep the same effect from happening in my own life and career?

In 1977, on a foggy runway in the Canary Islands, a KLM 747 and a Pan Am 747 collided. Tragically, 583 people died. It remains the deadliest aviation accident in history.

The KLM jet took off and clipped the top off the parked Pan Am jet. It tumbled down the runway, killing everyone on board. Amazingly, though, some of the passengers on the Pan Am 747 survived. How they survived is something that fascinates me.

In an instant, the Pan Am passengers found themselves sitting in a flaming cabin. But the survivors did something that the victims didn't: They got up and moved. A survivor said she watched a friend just sit there, frozen with terror. As the survivor leapt out of the cabin, she looking around, seeing dozens of people just sit there, burning to death. They were paralyzed by fear.

I've seen that phenomena in careers, too. People see things changing for the worse, but they just sit there hoping things will magically get better. They are terrified of the changes around them. They do the same thing over and over and expect different results (the definition of insanity, of course). And I've also seen people take the initiative and change before they end up becoming a statistic. This has happened over and over since the Great Recession began. What makes some people get busy and change while others sit and lose everything?

Newspaper editorial cartooning positions have nearly evaporated in the past decade (yes, I am very lucky to still be drawing and I know it). But that doesn't mean that I am going to sit still in fear. I'm going to experiment at *The Clarion-Ledger* with new ways for you to enjoy my work (thankfully I'm in an environment where that is encouraged). And I'm going to continue to do radio, speeches, books and other writing, too. I may fail. But it ain't going to be from sitting still. Because I know one thing for sure:

Change isn't scary. It's the grit that makes pearls.

a SOUTHERN THERMOMETER
IT'S COLD Y'ALL
WHINE 'BOUT IT ON TWITTER
AND ON FACEBOOK
MAKE GLOBAL WARMING JOKE.
BLAME AL GORE
HOARD BREAD and MILK
BE THANKFUL YOU DON'T LIVE UP NORTH.
DON'T GET OUT OF BED.
KNOW IT'LL BE 80° BY the WEEKEND.
MARSHALL RAMSEY

The Seaside Priest

The warm wind blew through the seaside bar on the warm Ash Wednesday morning. Palm trees gently swayed as a young college student sat next to an older gentleman. The man, an Episcopal priest, began talking to the student. The student, intent on drinking in as much as he could as quickly as he could, listened — but only about halfway. He had memories to obliterate.

The priest began to speak anyway:

"It's Ash Wednesday. You know, 'Ashes to ashes, dust to dust.' I spent the morning dusting and Lord knows, I have enough dust in my condo. And I have a couple of cremated pets on the shelf in urns. So I have some ashes. If you'd like to talk about my mortality, well that's another matter. I could fill your ear about it. But would you really care? Sure, I had a brush with death. But you don't care. I mean really, you can't get to my age without nearly dying once or twice. A drunk can weave into your lane. A tornado can hit your house. You can get stuck on a disabled cruise in the Gulf and have to eat onion sandwiches. And if you have experienced combat, death becomes a daily foxhole companion.

"No, I'm not going to bore you with my story. Because you don't want to hear it. Oh, you do? OK, it's cancer and I've nearly drowned. Big whoop. Both just made life a little clearer. I'd like to think the cancer was a pair of glasses. Nearly drowning was my progressive lenses: I can now see up close better than I could before.

"Ah, to be young and bullet-proof. Remember those days? That's right, you probably still do feel bulletproof."

The college student glared at the priest, who continued to talk anyway.

"I always feel sorry for teenagers who experience death first hand. They're robbed of their shield of protection. If I hadn't been naive at that age, I might not have tried new things. No, instead, I would have been in the fetal position until I was at least 40.

"Hang on a second, 'Bartender, could I have another iced tea?'"

"I gave up the drink a long time ago. I could see using it as a crutch during the bad times. And I had a pretty bad time for a while. I chose the Lord to lift me up instead. And do I mind if you smoke? Yes. You know those things will kill you. And me. And the bartender."

The bartender interrupted the priest's monolog. "Father, you want anything from the kitchen?"

"Yeah, Fred. Get me some oysters. And make it a double order. My friend here looks hungry."

The kid looked at the man in cutoffs and a black shirt with collar but didn't say anything.

"You might wonder why I am here in Paradise instead of somewhere more Hellish. Well, son, people need ministering everywhere. God put me here. And you seem to need some ministering."

The priest's tan revealed he had been "here" for a long time.

"Today is Ash Wednesday, son. You only have a brief time on this Earth. No one knows for sure — and isn't that a good thing? Can you imagine how freaked out if you knew when you were going to die? God did us a big favor on that one. But do God a favor: Treat each moment like the gift that it is. Obviously something is bothering you or you wouldn't have red eyes and be drinking so heavily."

The college student mumbled a few words under his breath.

The seaside priest acknowledged him and continued, "Yes, that is a tragedy. A terrible one. Life can be cruel. Yes, I know that it seems like God can be cruel, too. But you can't go down that road. You'll drive yourself crazy."

Dark clouds built on the horizon, making the green water even more vibrant from the contrast. A distant rumble of thunder announced the coming storm.

"We're OK here, son. It's fun to watch the lightning dance across the Gulf.

"Believe me, I haven't always been a man of the cloth. I suffered a tragedy much like yours. I lost everything in a sailing accident. An accident that was my fault, by the way. The last time I saw the woman I loved was as she drowned. So, yes, I understand your feeling about God being cruel. I understand what it is like to be eaten up by guilt."

The bartender brought the two orders of fried oysters as Jimmy Buffet's "Death of an Unpopular Poet" played on the jukebox.

"God isn't cruel. I personally think He is good. But I'm not going to get overly religious on you today. I'm just going to be here. My cancer? You want to hear about my cancer? Three doctors missed it. Should be dead. But I'm not. I'm here for a reason. Maybe it was to buy you oysters."

The college kid looked at the priest and smiled.

"When Christina drowned, my heart drowned, too. Never could love another woman. Why? There'd never be another woman like her. So I became a man of the cloth. The bad things in life shape us, son. Like rocks in a rushing stream. They smooth out the rough edges and make us shine. My accident pushed me in a new direction."

The storm's wind blew sand into the air. The priest watched the horizon, looking for waterspouts.

"The Gulf is a temperamental lady. I used to sail her all the time and never knew what mood she would be in. I screwed up and sailed us into a storm. Spent a week on a life raft after our boat sank. A passing shower and my ability to catch fish helped me survive. I'm still suffering from skin cancers from the sunburn I received. When the Coast Guard found me, I vowed to live the rest of my life to make up for my sin. I had to learn to ask for forgiveness for Christina's death. You will learn that, too."

The boy began to cry and spoke: "I didn't mean to cause the accident. I didn't mean for her to die."

"I know, son. I know. You have a heavy burden on your heart."

The priest walked over to an ashtray and dipped his finger in the cigar ashes.

"Sorry, these will have to do."

He wiped them on the boy's forehead and began to pray:

"Almighty God, you have created us out of the dust of the earth: Grant that these ashes may be to us a sign of our mortality and penitence, that we may remember that it is only by your gracious gift that we are given everlasting life; through Jesus Christ our Savior. Amen."

The seaside priest put his arm around the young man and held him tight. "I know you didn't mean to cause the wreck that killed my granddaughter. You are forgiven by me and by God."

A ray of sunshine broke through the dark clouds. A calm

fell across the water as the storm subsided. And on that Ash Wednesday, the seaside priest and the college student found peace beside a once-turbulent sea.

The Gift of HOPE

Hope is a word that gets thrown around a bunch these days. But I think we live in a time when really need more of it. H.O.P.E. stands for the four pillars of my life that help me get through my biggest struggles. Each letter stands for something that reduces stress and propels me through life.

H stands for Humor. It shouldn't shock you that I think that laughing at the things that drives you crazy is good medicine.

Immediately after my melanoma diagnosis, I nearly went crazy. When your own skin tries to kill you, it can and will stress you out. I think my parents realized that (they are both cancer survivors) and that may have had something to do with our family vacation that year. My sisters and their families joined my parents and my family in Destin, Florida. Of course, there is something inherently wrong with taking a skin cancer survivor to the beach, but I digress. While they were out on the beach, I was in watching Dr. Phil. I'm like a fork in microwave — I spark in the sun. So I avoid the direct sun during the middle part of the day.

About six that night, I decided to go for a swim. I took my shirt off and ran toward the surf. When I got there, there was a mom and two little girls swimming in the ocean. The mom noticed the six-inch scar on my back and stared right at it. It was big, red and ugly. Now, I'm not used to women staring at me (it doesn't happen often) so I felt self-conscious. Actually, I felt annoyed.

I had a choice. I could be ticked off or I could make a joke. I made a joke and have been telling the joke for 14 years.

She saw that I had noticed and felt embarrassed. I pointed at the scar and said, "Oh, this." She nodded sheepishly. I then said, "It was a shark attack and it happened right where your girls are playing."

She scooped up her girls and ran out of the water. My wife was over on the beach shaking her head.

That joke was an epiphany for me. I use the same techniques employed when I draw cartoons and apply them to my life. You will hear me making jokes. Sometimes they are inappropriate. But at the end of the day, they are my survival mechanism. H stand for Humor. Lord knows we could use a lot more of it in this world today.

O — Opportunity to serve.

I didn't tell anyone about my melanoma for about a year. In fact, I didn't even miss a cartoon. I'd work for three hours and sleep for six. I was determined to keep everything inside and push forward as if nothing had happened. But as I mentioned in the H part, I was falling apart inside. So one day, I wrote a column about my experience and how to detect a melanoma. Suddenly, my e-mail box filled with responses from people who said they were getting checked because they read my column.

The fourth doctor I went to found my melanoma. I was searching for a purpose for why I lived when so many hadn't.

It was at that moment, I found it. I was going to take the fight to the disease that had tried to kill me.

The Clarion-Ledger community room was full of cancer survivors. I had been named the Honorary Chairman for the American Cancer Society's Hinds County Relay for Life. As I stood there sipping my water, a fellow cancer survivor came up to me and said, "Thank God you just had skin cancer." It was that moment I realized that most people didn't realize how deadly melanoma really is. And with melanoma, early detection (and awareness) is the key.

Soon afterwards, my friend and coworker Keith Warren and I started Run from the Sun. It was an afternoon 5K race built around a free skin screening. I got busy getting on the radio and on the speaking circuit talking about sun safety.

I was given a blessing — the gift of life. I was doing everything I could to pay it forward.

Soon my fear began to fade like my scar.

One day I was driving down the interstate and tuned into a local sports radio program. I heard a caller talk about how he had heard my story and gone to get checked. The doctor found a melanoma that had started to spread. But he had been treated and was cancer free. He told how he had a chance to see his son grow up because of my story.

I pulled over and cried.

I don't know why I am here. Too many good people who had the same disease aren't. But serving others is helping me find the reason. And although it's not about me, I'm benefiting from it.

O is the opportunity to serve. It's about paying your gifts

forward.

P — Physical well-being

The sun peeked over the horizon, kissing the clouds and creating a red/orange blanket that covered the football field. But I didn't notice. I was pushing a board to the 20-yard line and back. Sweat poured down my face and my heart raced. From 5 a.m. until 6 p.m., I left my fat and sweat out on the football field during my bootcamp.

If this were a book, this chapter would be the longest. I can't stress enough how important physical well-being is to success in life. Virgil was right when he said, "The greatest wealth is health." I realized that when my own skin tried to kill me.

Just remember this: If you don't take care of your body, your body can't take care of you.

That involves diet, exercise and stress-reduction. You can't eat junk food and sit on the couch and expect long-term health. Eating a bowl full of pills isn't a good solution, either. It's expensive. And you generally feel like crap. And if you feel like crap, you don't have the energy to achieve great things.

Personally, I do an hour of aerobic/strength training four days a week and aerobic exercise two more days. I rest on Sundays. I also try to eat healthy. At this point, if I eat junk food or fast food (the same), I feel sluggish and rundown — like I put sugar in my gas tank. Oh yes, then there is sugar. I'm addicted to it and have made a real effort to cut it out of my diet. That's tough to do. Processed food is loaded with it. It's in those delicious, fizzy drinks. I've tried to find natural substitutes. I keep apples or bananas in my bag and eat a little snack every two hours to keep my blood sugar even. Since I'm active, I seek out complex carbohydrates. They give you a more even form of energy because the fiber involved slows your body's release of insulin. I have self-medicated with sugar before when I was down. That is a huge mistake because the crash afterwards leaves you craving more sugar.

It's a vicious cycle. One that once left me at 250 lbs. Today, I'm 210lbs. and eight inches smaller around the waist just from moderately monitoring my diet and exercising regularly.

Right after one of the most stressful times of my life, I got shingles. Then I got a melanoma. My body was telling me something! Stress kills your immune system and causes all kinds of problems from inflammation to heart and vascular damage. Our bodies can't handle being in the fight-or-flight mode 24/7. We have to learn how to unplug and unwind — and I know that's hard — I have three kids and eight careers! But exercise helps me some — and acts as a natural antidepressant. I'm also trying breathing exercises and meditation. Trust me, it's not easy to focus in this chaotic world we live in. But just know your life depends on it.

None of this is rocket science. We know what we have to do. But sometimes, it feels awesome to sit on the couch and eat ice cream. I think about the advice former football player turned actor Rosie Greer once gave about weight loss, "Instead of eating the whole cake, I eat one piece."

Take care of your body so it can take care of you.

E- E stands for Education

When I was diagnosed with a melanoma in-situ, I thought in-situ meant, "Buy coffin." It's Latin for "In place." My melanoma was still in the radial phase (growing outward, not downward) and was 100% curable. But I freaked out anyway because I didn't know that.

Imagine how much less stress I would have had if I had known what the terminology meant.

Of course, we have the internet. You can find any kind of knowledge that you want on the internet. Some is helpful, some isn't. So let me say that you have to educate yourself from reliable sources. I relied on my doctor, melanoma.org and several good books on the topic. I ate the topic up as if my life depended on it. Come to think of it, it DID depend on it.

My point is this: You have to be able to carry on a good conversation with your healthcare provider. Doctors aren't gods. They're brilliant people with more and more piled on their plate every single day. Same goes for mechanics, accountants, plumbers, etc. Whatever problem you have, you have to take charge. And educating yourself is the first step.

It also reduces your stress.

When I got the call for my malignant melanoma (a much more serious diagnosis than a melanoma in-situ), I was able to ask important questions that allowed me to quickly ascertain my situation. I knew my melanoma had been caught fairly early and my odds for 10-year survival were good. I knew the doctor was following the proper procedure and I understood what I was up against. Sure, I was worried. But not as worried as when I thought I was going to die from something 100% curable.

It's easy to go through life like a water bug skimming over the surface. But it's also an expensive and stressful way when things go awry. We have too much information at our fingertips now to remain in the dark. When things get bad, get busy learning. Knowledge is truly power. And acting on that knowledge will, as it did in my case, save your skin.

Visiting Hours

"Why are you still mad at me?"

"You know why."

"You hold a grudge."

"You would, too."

"It has been 30 years."

"Some things are unforgivable."

"You survived."

"You pushed the porta-potty I was in down the hill."

"I can't believe you can't get past that."

"I am still cleaning crap out of my ears."

The two brothers looked at each other and said nothing else. Their parents had an Olympic-sized gene pool and they had come from different ends. The oldest brother, Don, emerged from the deep end. Thoughtful and quiet, he was awkward in social settings. Rusty came from the fun end. His life was a big water-slide. If there was a crowd, Rusty would be in the middle of it.

The two men were like America. When times were good, they drove each other crazy. Their differences made them like sand in your shorts to each other. Honestly, they just annoyed each other. To Don, Rusty was an irritation. To Rusty, Don was stuffy and dull. But when things got bad, they worked together. Sometimes the most irritating sand makes the most beautiful pearls.

Today was one of those times.

"Think Mom will pull through this?" Rusty asked honestly.

Don looked at his brother and said, "I can't hear you. I have crap in my ears."

"Seriously. You think she will pull through this?"

They sat in the hospital as their mother sat in ICU. She had been in a coma for two weeks since her botched surgery.

"I don't know. I've called in three of my friends who are specialists. Even they are baffled why she won't wake up."

Don was a heart surgeon. He had helped guide his mother's care. But her weak heart had caused complications from the lung surgery. It gone from bad to worse.

Rusty looked at his older brother. He was tall, thin and slightly balding. He looked much like the photos they had seen of their father. That man had left when they were 10. At that point,

Don had become the man of the house and lost his childhood forever. Rusty almost felt sorry for his brother. Almost.

Don drank another sip of his coffee and looked at his younger brother. Eight years younger than he was, Rusty had golden hair and a white smile. He had made it big as a television personality in Denver and then transformed into an excellent novelist. As much as it pained Don to admit it, he was proud of his little brother. The kid was a great storyteller.

Together they were unstoppable. Unfortunately, that usually happened only during a crisis.

At the same time, both men sensed something wrong.

"Mom?" Rusty said.

Don paused and said, "No. It's him."

Both men turned to see an old man in the doorway of the hospital cafeteria. And old man who looked suspiciously like Don.

"You have a lot of nerve showing up now." Rusty growled.

The old man didn't say a word. He just stood there with tears in his eyes.

Rusty and Don stood up and walked over to confront him. It was as close to a Mexican standoff as the hospital would ever see.

"I have to see her. I'm so sorry for walking out on you. You're are such fine men. I've watched your careers from afar. But I have to see her."

"And that's the problem." Rusty said. "You had a lifetime to see her. But you screwed that up when you walked out on us."

Don just stood there, looking at his old man. The man who stole his childhood. The man whose absence had shaped him like a potter shapes a pot. He felt the rage boil inside him. He had never wanted to beat a man to death more than he wanted to at that moment. But he didn't. He closed his eyes and took a breath. There was someone bigger than him and he knew it. And she was lying in a coma upstairs in ICU.

"Come with me," Don said tersely.

The old man, stunned, followed sheepishly behind his two sons. Rusty had no idea what was going on, but sensed his brother had a plan.

He usually did. Except when the porta-potty rolled down the hill.

The nurses at the station saw the three men walking down the hall and started to tell them it wasn't visiting hours. But even they saw the purpose in Don's eyes.

Don grabbed his father by the neck and practically threw him in the room.

The old man limped over to the bedside and began to openly weep.

Both brothers stood there and watched their family be reunited for the first time in decades. And then their father began to speak.

"Lois, I don't know if you can hear me, but I am sorry. I know they are just words but my heart has been with you since I was a coward and walked out the door. The war had stolen my soul and I couldn't put you and the boys at risk any more. I got hooked on drugs and lived on the streets. I was a petty criminal and spent time and in and out of prison. But one day a man came and spoke to me. I swear I think he was an angel because his words rang in my heart. I cleaned up my life and began volunteering in his church. I prayed daily and stared at this crumpled picture of you and the boys. Remember those anonymous deposits you received at the bank? That was me. I began to rebuild my life but never could because you weren't in it. I don't expect you or the boys to forgive me. How could you? But I am going to ask you for it right here and right now."

Don, whose heart was petrified, felt his anger begin to melt. His eyes began to water. Rusty had lost it five minutes ago.

The old man held his old wife's hand and squeezed it.

And she squeezed his hand back.

My Cancer Story

I'm a Sagittarius, but I swear I was born under the sign of Cancer. Three of my grandparents had cancer. Both my parents are cancer survivors. And on April 17, 2001, I became one, too.

But mine is not a journey of great courage or grit. No, I'm sitting here because of the gift of early detection. My melanoma was caught by the fourth doctor who looked at me. And for nearly 14 years, I've tried to pay that gift forward.

I'm lucky to be here — and I know it.

In 2000, I was speaking to a friend who had recently survived melanoma. I thought melanoma was an Italian lounge singer — I knew nothing about the deadliest form of skin cancer other than that it came from moles. And I knew I had a lot of them. (I have dysplastic nevi syndrome) I had not gotten them checked in several years. I felt paranoid and after our conversation, I did what so many people did back in the day: I opened up the phone book and looked for a dermatologist.

I remember that appointment, but I don't remember the doctor's name. He looked at my back and I could see his eyes glaze over. It was like he was trying to count the stars. "Everything looks OK," he said and sent me on my way. But my inner-paranoid voice told me otherwise. I immediately had another doctor check me. He did a punch biopsy of a mole, which turned out to be a severely dysplastic nevi. On a scale of one to dead, it was about a six. So I followed up by going to another dermatologist. He said if I wanted to have that mole removed, I could go to a plastic surgeon. He handed me Dr. Kenneth Barraza's card.

And I promptly lost the card.

Thankfully my wife found it. She promptly kicked my butt to see Dr. Barraza. (I now know why married men live longer.) Dr. Barraza looked at my mole that had been punched and said, "That needs to come off immediately."

It had turned into a melanoma in-situ.

I thought "in-situ" meant "buy coffin." What it meant was that the melanoma was still in the radial phase and 100% curable. Yet, instead of being comforted, I panicked and asked that I be peeled with a potato peeler. I had six to eight moles cut off every six months.

A year later, Dr. Barazza saw a mole that looked odd to him

while I was on the table. It wasn't one he had planned to remove — but he did anyway. He cut it out and I didn't think anything else about it.

Tuesday, April 17, 2001, was the day of the Mississippi Flag election. People were mad about some of my cartoons and were calling me throughout the day. At 5:30 p.m., Dr. Barazza called and told me, "You have cancer." I laughed — it was the nicest call I had received all day.

Two days later, I woke up from surgery. My back still sports the scar from it.

But the most painful scar was the one on the inside. For a year, I didn't tell anyone I had had surgery. I nearly went crazy from the fear. Melanoma is an aggressive cancer. And it likes to come back. I had to learn how to cope.

A few months later, my family went to Destin (yes, I went to the beach!). Around 6 p.m., I went for a swim. A lady and her two girls were staring at my scar. I smiled and said, "Oh that, it's a shark attack and it happened where your daughters are swimming." She ran out of the water (it was the summer of the shark, after all) and I found the peace I was looking for. It was that trip that I developed H.O.P.E. (Humor, Opportunity to Serve and Physical well-being and Educate Yourself). And hope has keep me going since.

Yesterday, I had my 76th mole biopsied. Yes, I am nervous as I await yet another report. But I will continue to appreciate each sunrise. And I will try to share the blessing I've been given. I know how lucky I am to still be alive. And I will continue to raise awareness as long as I am on this side of the grass.

What's the moral of my story? Take control of your health. Get your skin screened. Why? I want you to have the blessing I received.

I tell people that good things come from bad moments. And in my case, cancer was a blessing. It woke me up and allowed me the opportunity to help others.

I can live with that.

IT'S TIME to GIVE the SOUTH A TASTE OF SUMMER!
ATTIC FAN

When Hell Turns to Paradise

As the small ship cut through the light surf, Franklin Hudson scanned the horizon for Hell. His ancient eyes were as blue as the surrounding sea. He stood on the bow, watching the tropical island loom on the horizon. Salt spray lashed his leathery skin. A handful of Cumulonimbus clouds exploded into the sky, looking like volcanic sentinels guarding the little spit of coral.

The old man was thankful that it was only the clouds guarding it.

"You ever been here before?" the tanned German tourist standing next to him asked in passable English.

"Once. A long time ago."

"Did you come to dive? The diving is world class here. That's why I'm here."

The old man grinned at the young man's innocence. He had been born during a time of peace. Peace earned by the old man's generation.

"Not exactly. I did spend a short time in the water. But I was on land most of the time."

"When were you here last?"

The old man was going to answer, "Every night in my nightmares," but gave a simpler, more direct answer.

"September 15, 1944."

The German tourist's eyes opened. "Oh. You were in the war?"

"Yes. As a Marine. I was in the war. And the war is still in me."

The old man rubbed his leg, where shrapnel still resided, and continued, "I've heard the diving is spectacular here. I hope you have a good trip."

The young man smiled and said, "Thank you. My great grandfather was in the war, too. I'm glad you two never met."

The old man smiled again. He liked the kid's sense of humor. "Me, too. Is he still alive?"

"Nein. He died in the war. Was killed when his Messerschmitt 109 was shot down over France. My great grandmother was never the same after that. She hates you Yanks."

"I understand completely," he said as he patted the kid on the back. "I understand completely."

The old man thought of the conversation he had participated in last week.

"YOU CAN'T GO! YOU ARE 88 years old. There is no way I will allow you to make a trip like that alone." The dark-haired, middle-aged woman stood with her hands on her hips.

"If the Imperial Japanese Army can't stop me, you can't either. I changed your diaper. You and your mother and even your grandmother couldn't keep me from going. I have something important to do. And if you'll excuse me, I'm going to do it." He picked up a small container, gathered tickets and looked at the destination on the paper.

He was headed back to Peleliu Islands.

Franklin Hudson had never mentioned his part in World War II to his family. But on the day he turned 85, he began to open up about it. The family had known not to wake him from a deep sleep and knew he would have terrifying nightmares, but they were horrified to hear what hell he had seen in his life. The retired elementary school principal had seen and done things in the name of his country that no man should ever have to do. But he did them. He did out of loyalty to his country, Corps and companions. Franklin Hudson, a meek man by nature, was a trained killer who had helped win World War II. And after the war, he suppressed it deep inside his torn soul.

Now, on the sunset of his life, he was going to let it all go in the only place he could.

"Welcome to Peleliu!" the young, tanned lady greeted him at the dock. "Are you Mr. Franklin Hudson?"

The old man nodded. He could smell familiar smells.

"Very good. If you will sit here, I will call your tour guide. Welcome back Mr. Hudson. And on behalf of the residents of Peleliu, thank you."

"I have to admit," he smiled as he sat," this is a much warmer greeting than the last time I was here."

He looked over at the Japanese tourists sitting over in the corner. They probably had lost a loved one here, too. A slight flicker of hatred boiled up in his heart, but was quickly extinguished. Time had healed that wound (although he still had yelled at his granddaughter when she had bought a Mitsubishi TV. "THEY BUILT THE PLANE THAT KILLED MY

FELLOW MARINES!" he screamed at the young girl. There were still some of those planes in the jungle near the airfield he had captured.) In hindsight, they hadn't even needed to capture the island. Nearly 1,800 Americans had paid the ultimate price to help cover General Douglas MacArthur's effort to retake the Philippines. He looked over at the Japanese tourists again. Some 20,000 of their countrymen had died here as well. Franklin nodded at the tourists. Their families had suffered, too.

The heat and humidity was like a thick, wet coat smothering his soul and as bad as he remembered it. He had never been that thirsty before or since. In preparation for the invasion, the Japanese had poisoned the watering holes. The only water he had for the first couple of days tasted like the oil barrels it came ashore in — when he got water at all. This time he came prepared. He had a bag full of water and a small container. He took out his handkerchief and wiped the sweat from his wrinkled brow. He hadn't sweated like this since New Orleans, his childhood home.

He had made one friend while growing up in the Crescent City. His name was Johnny Morton and they lived next door to each other on St. Charles Avenue in the Garden District. Franklin and Johnny had everything in common. Both were sons of college professors. Both were excellent students and athletes. And both had signed up for the U.S. Marine Corps the day they turned 18. They were going to kill Japs, the very nonpolitically correct word they used back in 1943.

By a twist of fate, they were together that day as the landing craft stormed ashore. Franklin remembered Johnny throwing up. He remembered how pale his face was. He remembered their scrambling over the side of the boat into the warm, tropical water. He could see the blood flowing in currents around the boat. And he remembered the Japanese bullet tearing into Johnny's head. As he ran toward the airfield, he turned one last time to see his friend twitching on the sand. Franklin Hudson never saw Johnny Morton, his best friend in the whole world, again.

Fate and two feet had spared his life.

The car stopped near the ocean. The guide said, "The Marines landed at 08:32 on 15 September; the 1st Marines to the north on "White Beach…" The old man looked at him distantly and said, "I know. I was there."

The island looked different now. Vegetation, blasted by Naval gunfire and napalm, had grown back. Hunks of iron were now rusting into history — much like the other survivors and himself. Franklin felt his blue eyes water. Moisture streamed down his wrinkled face.

There it was. The very place where he had come ashore.

"Excuse me."

The guide stopped and said, "yes?"

"I'd like to take a moment and walk on the beach. I have a few things I'd like to do."

The guide, recognizing a moment to smoke a cigarette said, "Sure," and helped the old man out of the car.

The path was worn. The calm water lapped and tickled the land. Franklin wiped his forehead again and took a long sip of water from a water bottle. He got his bearings and walked down the beach about 25 yards. He sighed and sat down, feeling the warm sand on his bottom.

"I was hoping you'd return."

A lone figure walked down from the beach from the opposite direction.

"I couldn't leave you."

"But you did."

"You were dead the second the bullet hit you. My sergeant was screaming for me to move. I had to keep going."

Johnny Morton sat next to his old friend and then put his arm around him.

"You've really gotten old."

"And you look the same. I see you every night in my nightmares."

"I know. I visit you every night. I haven't found peace."

Both men sat, watching a storm brew in the distance.

"We won the battle and the war. I went home and married Juliet Jenkins. You remember her from high school — the cute blond that sat in Mr. Cummings' Math class. We had three kids and they each had two. I went to Tulane and then worked as an elementary school principal and moved to Marietta, Georgia. New Orleans flooded a few years ago from a hurricane. You wouldn't have believed the chaos. Juliet died ten years ago from cancer."

Johnny Morton sat silently.

"To answer the question you haven't asked: Yes it was worth it. Our country became great because of sacrifices like yours. I miss you, Johnny. We all missed you. Your girlfriend Samantha went on to marry another man, but I know she didn't love him like she loved you. She named her first son John."

A tear streamed down the ghost's face.

"I've traveled halfway around the world to be with you today. I'll be with you permanently soon. Time is about to do what the Japanese couldn't. Like you, I'll be history. But like you, I won't be forgotten."

Franklin stood up, pulled a small container out of his bag and walked to the water's edge. There he sprinkled ashes into the sea.

Johnny smiled. "Thank you, friend."

"Happy Memorial Day, Johnny."

And at that moment, Hell transformed into Heaven. And Franklin Hudson helped an old friend find peace at last.

The Actor

God could not have created a more perfect morning. The sun rose over the Malibu hills, casting warm sunbeams on the large beach house. A white seagull floated on the breeze, doing his morning aerial dance before scrounging for breakfast. The Hollywood star pulled a chair up on his deck. He watched the waves crash on the beach, enjoying their calming effect. As last night's alcohol died in his system, he felt his head began to throb.

"I've got to stop drinking." His friendship with Jack Daniels made his head spin. It was a Hollywood tradition: Murder your body at night and then go healthy during the day. No time for a beach jog. Maybe a sprout shake or some suppository vitamins would make him feel better. Although he had lived in Los Angeles for 25 years, he still felt like a stranger in a foreign land.

He picked up the most recent copy of the trade magazine *Variety*. His latest picture, *Attack on the White House,* was No. 1 at the box office. The review had called him "the next Tom Cruise."

"Oh Lord," he bemoaned to the gull who had landed on his porch. "I hope not. The moment I jump on Oprah's couch, I'm moving back to Mississippi."

Cole Rayborn was a $25-million-dollar-a-picture Hollywood star. But all the fame and wealth still left him empty. Yes, he had his people: Agents, security, staff — all the folks a multimillionaire actor needs. But he didn't have friends. Well, other than Jack Daniels. And that wasn't exactly a mutual friendship.

The gull cocked his head, curious as to why the man hadn't at least given him a French Fry. Gulls don't worry about silly things like friends. They just worry about where their next meal is coming from.

Cole picked up his iPad and flipped to his hometown paper. He liked to peruse the local news, keeping tabs on old friends and loved ones. The past 25 years had been rough on his old home city. Middle-class flight had left the tax base much smaller. Now, only the uber rich and the very poor lived there. And his parents. They still lived in the small house where he grew up.

That was a source of embarrassment to him. He had tried to give them money for a new house, but they were proud. Stubborn, actually. His father had worked for the State of Mississippi and his mom had been a teacher. Both were retired now and lived for their 13th retirement check. The fact that their son was one of the richest actors on earth was a source of pride for them. "You're the only person I know who knew what he was going to do when he was 8 and actually did it," his father had said at the Academy Awards. His favorite photo was his mother kissing his Best Actor Oscar statue. But they wouldn't take his money. "Just keep doing us proud, boy. That's reward enough."

The National Tattler had once gone to Mississippi and taken pictures of their little house and painted him as a cheapskate. "Cole plays while his parents suffer." The tabloids always had a way to find the cloud in every silver lining. Making people look like buttheads sold more copies. It just sucked when it was you they used you to boost circulation.

But that was part of the game. With great wealth comes great scrutiny — even from jerks.

He flipped through the iPad and read the headlines. "Baggy Pants Ban." He rolled his eyes. "House votes on Charter Schools." OK. "Fabled drama teacher dies in car wreck."

Cole dropped the iPad onto the deck, shattering the glass.

It takes one special teacher to change your life. Lenore Gabriel was that teacher. While the other kids wanted to play football, Cole wanted to act. He sought out the small drama club in his high school and met Miss Gabriel. She changed his life forever. He hung on her every word. He was clay in her hands. Now, at the age of 55, those beautiful hands had been stilled.

As the gull watched, one of the toughest men in Hollywood broke down and cried.

"FLIGHT 43 to Atlanta final boarding call."

Delta could get there but you had to go through Atlanta. In fact, the old joke was that when you died, you had to got through ATL to get to Heaven or Hell. Cole wore his sunglasses and an overcoat as he sat in First Class. He stirred his drink with a straw, thinking about why he was flying back home.

Home. The one place that could make him feel whole again. God, it had been so long. He hadn't even called his parents. He just hopped the first flight he could find. (He thought about chartering a private jet, but not on this trip.) He was going home as Cole Rayborn, Mississippian, not Cole Rayborn, actor.

"Aren't you?..." the flight attendant began. Cole smiled and said, "I'm afraid so."

The flight attendant blushed and asked for his autograph. Cole smiled and said, "Sure."

By the time he arrived in Jackson, the airport was deserted. He went up to the rent-a-car desk and said, "The smallest car you have." The young girl looked up and nearly fainted.

Thirty minutes later, after knocking on the door, he was startled when his dad came to the door with a gun. "BOY, I could have shot you! Do you know what time it is? Do you know how to call?"

The old man's protests stopped, though, and he set the pistol down. He hugged his son as tight as he could. "It's so good to see you, boy." Cole's mother ran into the room and nearly tackled her child.

It was a cold and cloudy morning at St. Saints Episcopal church. Cars lined the oak-filled neighborhood as the mourners filed into the nave. "Episcopalians put on great weddings and funerals," Cole thought. But he would have traded his fortune to see Miss Gabriel again.

He took a seat in the back as the service progressed. Former and present students stood up and told the packed house how much their teacher had meant to them. The love could have lifted the roof that morning. And at the very end, a lone man walked to the front of the room. He knelt down and laid across the coffin. Cole Rayborn, the toughest man in Hollywood, broke down and openly wept for the woman who had given him his start.

The mourners gasped when they realized who the hulking man in the front of the room was. Cole walked up to the pulpit and pulled out a piece of paper.

"A teacher is a precious gift to a child. This particular teacher changed my life and made me who I am today. In this era of teaching to the test, the arts are under siege in our schools. Today, with the help of the Mississippi Arts Commission, I'm setting up the Lenore Gabriel scholarship fund for teachers who want to pursue teaching the arts. And I'm donating even more money to make sure the drama program survives at my old school.

"Miss Gabriel changed my life. Now it is time for me to pay that forward."

Cole folded the paper and put it in his suit pocket. He

walked past the coffin and stopped again. He bent over and kissed it one last time.

"Thank you, Miss Gabriel. God sent you to me. Now He has called you home."

And as he stood up, the sun broke through the clouds, illuminating the church's expensive stained glass. The people in the room and the coffin were bathed in a warm light.

It was Cole Rayborn's finest performance. And for the first time in 25 years, the actor felt whole.

The Little Book of Courage

My leap of faith began from paradise. I had a great job, amazing bosses, fantastic coworkers and I lived in San Diego, California — a city with the finest weather in the United States. A southern voice on my answering machine had offered me a job — my dream job.

It was nearly November and I had just come back from the beach.

Without hesitation, I dialed the number and accepted the job. Soon, I would be the new editorial cartoonist in Jackson, Mississippi starting on December 16, 1996. My wife shot me a look like, "I hope you know what you are doing." I shot her a look back that replied, "Me, too."

Most of what I knew about Mississippi emanated from books and, unfortunately, Hollywood. I had been through the state on my way out West — that was when I got the first rock ding in my windshield. I remember traveling down I-10 thinking, "This is where Camille hit." Sure, I was from Atlanta — but that didn't count. I needed to do my homework. And needed to start immediately.

I walked from our apartment down Washington Avenue to the local library. I asked for all the books they had on Mississippi and the librarian returned with a whopping two books. One was a book on the general history of Mississippi. The other was a biography of Medgar Evers.

I sat in our living room reading Evers' story. A cool sea breeze rattled the blinds as a seagull went by. Heck, a 747 could have flown by and I wouldn't have noticed. I started reading parts of it aloud to my wife. Courage. Love. A desire to make his home better for his children. I think I read the book in an afternoon. Then I reread it.

Last night, I presented the courage award at a scholarship banquet in Medgar's honor. Myrlie was there. His brother Charles, too. And I got to meet some of his kids and several of his nieces and nephews. I leaned over to his nephew Carlos and said, "I'd imagine your family reunions are amazing." People who knew and loved Medgar were standing at the podium, telling stories about their friend 52 years after he was assassinated. He came alive again in the Hilton hotel.

When the banquet was over, I briefly spoke to actor Dan Ackroyd. He went on about his love of Mississippi and how more people needed to know about it. I agreed whole-heartedly. I heard the same excitement in his voice that I've had for the past 20 years.

I leapt from paradise when I came here. But I found a different kind of paradise when I landed. It's more flawed. It's a land of challenge and courage. One that shapes you into a better person.

Soon, I'm visiting Washington, D.C. I'm taking my sons through the Arlington Cemetery. I want to show them where heroes guard freedom for eternity. And somewhere in that garden of stones, we'll find Medgar Evers' grave.

I thought about that biography last night and how it made my evening so special. A leap of faith requires courage. And I learned it from a man who died a long time ago.

The Bespectacled Man

Jimmy Bob Bullosk oozed misery and reeked of hate. He was a modern-day Grinch with a heart three-times too small. You see, he was a bully. He picked on the weak. And he mocked the helpless. For 23 years, he had left broken spirits and noses in his wake. But today, on the eve of his 24th birthday, Jimmy Bob was about to learn the meaning of empathy.

It had started at an early age with Jimmy Bob. When he was six, he tripped the little girl in church, causing her to bust her chin and bleed on her new dress. Jimmy Bob thought that was hilarious. He had spilled the milkshake on the special-needs child in the cafeteria. He taunted the little boy by mispronouncing his name until the boy cried. It would be fair to say that Jimmy Bob was a jerk. But some would call him something much stronger.

Jimmy Bob lived and worked in the tiny Mississippi town of Bucksburg. One Tuesday afternoon, while walking home from his construction job , he saw a small, bespectacled man crossing the street.

"Hey F****T!" he called out the gay slur so people as far away as Jackson could hear it.

The man looked around, like he didn't know what was going on.

"Yeah, I'm talkin' to you q***r!" Jimmy Bob launched another slur at the unsuspecting man.

"You talking to me?" the man asked in a very un-De Niro-like way.

Jimmy Bob felt the rush of endorphins he got when he picked on someone weaker than himself.

The bespectacled man, who was just passing through Bucksburg, looked up at the large man walking his way. Jimmy Bob towered over him when they met in the middle of Main Street. The man tried to walk around the hulking bully, but every time he moved, Jimmy Bob moved in the same direction, blocking him.

"Um, excuse me," the bespectacled man said politely.

Jimmy Bob laughed and knocked the man's hat off his head. He then pushed his folder of papers out of his arms, causing a blizzard of forms on the ground.

The bespectacled man just looked at Jimmy Bob without emotion. He looked back down at his paper and said, "I really wish you hadn't done that."

Jimmy Bob laughed. And then he took a swing at the man, aiming right for the bespectacled man's spectacles.

In a quickness that was unhuman, the bespectacled man grabbed Jimmy Bob's hand and stopped it in mid-punch. He then said something that Jimmy Bob couldn't understand and a shock of electricity traveled into the hulking bully's body. Jimmy Bob fell to the ground and began to seize.

As he lay on the ground flopping around, Jimmy Bob relived every incident where he had bullied another person. Except this time it was much different. Jimmy Bob felt the other person's pain.

He tripped the little girl in church again, causing her to bust her chin and bleed on her new dress. He began to cry and feel shame. He felt the searing pain of the chin wound. He once again spilled the milkshake on the special-needs boy in the cafeteria. But he felt the humiliation as the cold chocolate ran down his back and the other kids laughed. Jimmy Bob rolled on the ground in pain as he saw him arguing with his young wife. He punched her in the face. But this time, it was Jimmy Bob's teeth that fell out as he lost consciousness.

The bespectacled man looked down at the broken bully and said, "I am the answer to many of your victims' prayers. I was sent to teach you a lesson. I pray you've learned it." He then reached into his coat and placed a card on the bully's cheek. On it was golden printing that read:

Thou shalt love thy neighbour as thyself. There is none other commandment greater than these.

The bespectacled man looked up to the sky and said, "Mission accomplished, Boss." Then, he smiled and disappeared.

HOW WE LEARN GEOGRAPHY IN the SOUTH...
TORNADO WARNING: YOKNAPATAWPHA COUNTY...
UH OH.
MAP
MARSHALL RAMSEY

The Ballad of Alex Littlewinker

Had a guy in a Nissan SUV riding my bumper this morning on my commute. I started to get mad – but I learned a long time ago not to allow the person behind you to dictate your driving.

So I made up a story for him instead.

His name is Alex Littlewinker. He didn't do particularly well in school and he failed shop. Unfortunately he lost three fingers and had to have a plate put in his head. This morning, he was in a hurry because he has a really bad case of itchy anal glands and can't sit for long periods of time due to his eyes bleeding from the intense itching. He was on his way to UMMC where he was going to get a flashlight-sized suppository to cure the itching – needless to say, he was in a big, big hurry.

Thankfully Mr. Littlewinker managed to get around me on the interstate but was unfortunately foiled once again by all the other drivers who were choosing to only drive 15 miles over the speed limit.

I wish Mr. Littlewinker well. And I hope he finds relief for his eye-bleeding anal itching soon.

Riding Out the Storm

A cold rain poured down on New Orleans. Simon O'Mally looked out his window at the city and caught caught a glimpse of his reflection. "How did I get this old?" he thought in disgust. Sex, drugs and rock and roll had somehow turned into Viagra, ibuprofen and easy listening. This was no way for an aging rockstar to live.

But was he really alive? It felt more like he had died years ago.

He breathed against the glass. A fog formed. "OK," he thought, "At least I am alive." He just wished he could have said the same for his career.

Tonight, he'd stand on stage with his guitar and play his hits from 30 years ago to a crowd who would show up fashionably late and talk through all the new songs. They might cheer his biggest hit, a No. 2 smash from 1986 – the one that was playing in the damned elevator. Or they might leave early because of the weather. He looked at his phone and saw three messages from his manager. Simon replied by throwing the phone across the room. He was throwing an epic pity party in his small hotel room. No one else was invited.

Simon felt the wrinkles on his face. Was this all that was left? He imagined himself diving out the window and onto the street below. That might get him on the charts again. Death did Elvis' career wonders.

No. He wouldn't quit. An old freighter pushed against the Mississippi River's mighty current. It struggled and sent up a frothing wake. But it was heading toward its destination. It didn't stop because things were "too hard." Simon thought of a day from his youth. He and his father were sailing near Sydney, Australia, when a sudden storm came up. "I'm scared, Dad! I want off!" His father, who was fighting to keep the ship afloat, screamed back, "Then jump overboard. But I'm not quitting. We have a beautiful destination ahead of us. We just have to ride out the storm!"

His father died three years later of a heart attack. But they didn't die that day. They kept fighting all the way back to their destination. Simon thought of all the beautiful destinations he had seen since then: MTV, award shows, beautiful fans, exotic cities. If he had quit that day, he would have missed them all.

I just have to ride out the storm!

New Orleans is a city of lost souls. But one of those souls also became Simon's muse. He walked over to the desk and started writing lyrics. Images of a storm flowed from his hand. Images of a boat and a small boy. Currents swirled around the green water. Froth churned in the storm. Sea-spray stung his eyes. And by the end of the lyrical journey, hope and grit arrived safely at their destination. It was a song he needed to write. It was a song he needed to hear. He picked up his guitar and the melody flowed from his fingers. Never had a song been this easy to write. Never had he felt magic.

"Thanks, Dad."

That night in the House of Blues, Simon O'Mally played to a 3/4 house. They showed up late and talked during his newer songs. But when he played, "Riding out the Storm" at the end of the last encore, you could hear a pin drop. "This is for my dad," he said as he began to play. Camera phones rose like the tide, capturing the raw moment when an aging rock star delivered three and half minutes of magic to the world. When his guitar's last string silenced, the hall erupted into cheers. Simon wiped the sweat off his forehead and the houselights came on.

"Helluva song, Simon!" his manager nearly tackled him. "I was even inspired by it. Where did that come from?"

Simon tapped his heart and pointed to the sky.

Postscript.

"Riding out the Storm" became a YouTube sensation. It was the most retweeted video of 2015 and was shared over and over on Facebook. Like the 1,000th match hitting wet wood, a fire was started with that song. And Simon O'Mally had his first No.1 song ever. It was played at the Super Bowl the next year and became the theme song for anyone facing a struggle. When Simon came back to New Orleans the next year (to a packed house), he met a man and his daughter. "I was going to kill myself, but I heard your song. You helped me ride out the storm. Now she has a dad and I have hope. Thank you."

Simon O'Mally hugged the man and the little girl. And at that moment, he realized, he also had ridden out the storm.

The Little Things

It's really the little things that make the biggest impressions.

Like a cricket, for instance.

My family walked into the National World War II Museum in New Orleans on Sunday. The first thing we noticed when we walked through the doors was a giant plane suspended from the ceiling. The Douglas C-47 had the same paint scheme it would have worn on D-Day. It was an impressive display.

Then we saw a much smaller display — an older man (who was probably well into his 80s) sitting behind a small table. He beckoned us over and asked my sons, "You boys know what a cricket is, don't you?"

My boys stood there quietly for a second, trying to figure out what the trick was to his question. As the standoff continued, I noticed an 82nd Airborne pin on his collar.

"You were in the 82nd Airborne?" I asked. I knew he had jumped out of a plane similar to the one above us.

"I'm still in the 82nd Airborne," he quickly replied with a grin. He then focused his attention back to my sons.

"So, you boys know what a cricket is?"

My middle son asked, "A bug?"

The volunteer smiled and said, "Yes. But it is much more. Imagine you've jumped into Normandy on D-Day. It's night and a man comes toward you. You have to find out if he is friend or foe. You can't just ask him. So you take this out and do this."

He pulled out a small brass device and clicked it once.

"You're separated, hungry and nervous. You're lost. You need to find your friends. And if he is one of your friends, he will do this."

He then clicked the clicker twice. The little device made a sound that sounded like a mechanical cricket.

"Now, what happens if he doesn't reply?"

My son suggested, "You shoot him?"

The volunteer said matter-of-factly, "Yes, you kill him before he kills you."

My sons all held the cricket and clicked it themselves. As they did, they could see the man in front of them jumping out of that giant plane. They walked a mile in his paratrooper boots. They understood D-Day a little better. He morphed from a senior citizen into a hero.

We toured the museum and were impressed by the big exhibits. We loved the B-17 Flying Fortress and the Sherman tank. And the Tom Hanks 4-D movie was amazing. But it was the little things that gripped us: The last letter written by a Marine on the day he was killed. The Kbar knife with a bullet hole in the handle (that saved a Marine's life). The telegram informing a mother that she had lost her precious son. The oral histories of how average Americans coped during the war. Two actual Medals of Honor. Hattiesburg Medal of Honor recipient Jack Lucas' wallet. The display of soldiers that showed how few troops the U.S. had at the beginning of World War II compared to those in Japan and Germany.

Five hours later, we walked out and the hero had gone home. I know we'll probably never see him again. But for a brief moment, a World War II paratrooper and his cricket allowed us to understand history a little better.

Because it really is the little things that make the biggest impressions.

Update: The National World War II Museum announced today (1/15/15) that Tom Blakey has joined so many of his fellow World War II veterans in the great beyond. God bless a great man who brought World War II to life.

The Farmer

When I travel to speeches, I always chose the fastest and most direct route. That's because I'm usually late, burning time and flying like a bat out of a Justin Bieber concert. But not this particular morning. I was driving to Natchez, Mississippi, the beautiful southern town perched on the bluff of the Mississippi River. And for once, I had the time to enjoy the trip. The crisp, cobalt-blue sky stretched across the horizon, kissing the trees. The previous night's storms had rinsed the pollen out of the air and left the world cleansed. The colors were absolutely vivid. New leaves cloaked the world with a blanket of bright.

I had taken the long way.

And by the long way, I mean the Natchez Trace Parkway. The Natchez Trace follows along the path of the old road from Natchez to Nashville. Traveled by river men and thieves in the 1800s, the two-lane road now cuts through some of Mississippi's most breathtaking countryside. My drive gave me time to decompress (since you can only drive 50 mph on it or Mr. Park Ranger will give you a hefty federal ticket). It also gave me time to think about some things in my life that were getting me down.

Life had recently thrown some pretty frustrating setbacks my way. I knew something had to change, but I didn't know what. I also knew I couldn't keep doing the same things over and over and expect different results. That's the definition of insanity, after all. And I was about to go insane. After a while you have to conclude that your problems just might be caused by yourself. My ego was battered like a ping pong ball in a tornado. My life was adrift.

I like giant oak trees. I run past one every Saturday and find them to be inspiring spots for pondering And about halfway between Jackson and Clinton, there's a massive one on the edge of a huge plowed field. I spotted it, pulled my car over and hiked toward it with an apple in hand. As I climbed through the barbed-wire fence, it seemed like a perfect spot to take a break.

I quickly got lost in my thoughts and the beautiful morning.

A rude shout jolted me back to reality.

"HEY! YOU! YOU AREN'T SUPPOSED TO BE HERE!"

The shouts came from an old pickup truck that had appeared

on a dirt road about 25-yards to my West.

"I SAID,YOU ARE TRESPASSING!"

I must have missed the sign when I went through the fence. I sure missed the truck pulling up.

A man got out of the truck. He wasn't particularly tall but stood straight as an arrow. His snow white hair contrasted with his dark skin. Instead of brown eyes, he had vivid green irises. He could have been 60 or 90. All I know is that he walked with a confidence that was hard to miss. And that confidence was coming toward me.

"I'm sorry," I said apologetically. "I just saw this tree and it looked like a good place to take a break."

The man, seeing I wasn't a poacher, axe murderer or thief, dropped his guard. He stuck out his hand and said, "My name is Ralph. This is my farm — and my tree. And you are right, it is a great place to take a break. It's where I eat lunch when I'm out working."

I offered him half my apple and he took a seat next to me. We talked for a few minutes and he started asking me a slew of questions. I, of course, told him my life story. Any more whine and I would have owned a vineyard.

He smiled and said, "You know, you sure are like me when I was your age." I was hoping he'd share when that was; he didn't.

"See this land? My father gave it to me. And his father to him and so on. I started farming it when I was in my 20s and I'll be honest, it was a disaster. Weeds, bugs, drought, rain, storms all killed the crops. And I blamed everyone but myself. I thought all I had to do was throw some seed out in the fertile soil and I'd reap an amazing crop. Sometimes I did. But most of the time, it was a failure. There were some years when the weeds grew higher than the corn."

I nodded out of kindness, but not seeing the relevance, I was kind of lost. I'm dense like that sometimes.

"Anyway, one day I was under this very tree and had an epiphany. You do know what an epiphany is, don't you?" I nodded and showed off my public education. He continued, "I began planning my farm and farming my plan. I worked hard in the fields. When I had a bumper crop, I saved for a bad year. Come on, I want to show you something." He hit me on the back and we stood and walked to a corner of his field. There was a giant vegetable garden. "This, though, is when I truly became a successful farmer."

I looked at the plot of land and kind of shrugged my shoulders.

"You know whose crops these are?"

I answered, "Yours?"

He chuckled, "Nah. They are the people's in the nearby town. I donate a portion of my field for a community garden. It's a way to give my blessing back. To, as they say, pay it forward."

I admired the plants coming up through the rich, dark soil.

But, not seeing the obvious message here, I said, "So what's this all have to do with your succeeding?"

The farmer stood tall and said, "Your heavenly Father gave you a patch of land, too. It's called life. It's fertile and you can grow any crop on it you want. But you've been like I was: You've been farming without a plan. Weeds like depression and laziness have taken your rich soil over. It's time for you to clear your fields and start farming with a purpose. Have a plan. Weed your plot. Plant purposeful seeds. Save for a rainy day — because bad seasons will happen. But when they do, don't blame outside factors for your woes. Praise the good and the bad. And most importantly, reserve some of your farm to help others. That's why we're here."

He smiled as the lightbulb came on my head.

I'm not sure why I traveled that way that day. But I have to believe it was to bump into Ralph the farmer. As we walked back to his truck and my car, he smiled and said, "Here's my number. Next time you're down this way, I'll buy you lunch."

I laughed and said, "Nah, I owe you."

He smiled and said, "Hey, you've already given me half an apple. But just remember this — Plan your farm and farm your plan. And then you'll grow an amazing crop."

FUN WITH CANCER SCARS No.124
Oh, the scar you're rudely staring at? Shark Attack. Right where your girls are...

The Adventure

How do you turn a fun fishing trip into a battle for survival?

Just add water.

Lots of water. Lots of rushing, clear, cold water. Also, you need a rootball from an old tree. Mix in a swift current that grabs your 20-ft. boat and flips it when it slams against the snag, and presto.

In less than 30 seconds, the boat was sinking. I scrambled to get my son onto the part of the boat that was above the surface. Then I grabbed the keys and phone out of my pants pockets and got them in my jacket's upper pockets before they got wet. My friend Jim, who was driving the boat, hung onto the back, securing what he could and fighting to keep from being swept downstream himself. Jim and I made sure my son's lifejacket was secure. Check. Water pushed against the boat and scoured the river bottom, quickly making it too deep for me to touch. All three of us remained remarkably calm.

We watched as the contents of our boat floated downstream.

On the sandbar nearby were three people fishing — two guys and a girl. I guess you can say that guardian angels sometimes own rod and reels. The two men sprang into action and hopped into their boat. They chased our stuff and gathered it, placing it safely on the sandbar. I called them over and rescued my son from the top of the boat. I handed them my jacket — the keys and the phones were soon safe, too. They then came and picked Jim up. He was in a dangerous position and was at risk of being swept loose by the current.

I slipped down and tried to dislodge the boat. The cold water was beginning to make me shiver (thankfully we were in the warmer, calmer Buffalo River and not the White River, which was 52 degrees and had a much swifter current.) The two guys came over to the boat and the three of us started to try to dislodge it. That's when I slipped and the current caught me in its grasp.

What happened next was pure panic.

There was a drag chain on the front of the boat. It was a small stretch of chain tied to a long rope, designed to slow the boat as one fishes. Somehow, it had gotten wrapped around my leg. As I got swept away from the rocking boat by the current, the line pulled tight, snapping my ankle. I can best describe what happened next as what it must feel like to be waterboarded.

Paul LaCoste's Fit4Change became a Godsend. I did the mother of all sit-ups as I struggled to keep my head above the water. And then I reached the chain and started to try to unwrap it from my throbbing ankle. It must have taken a few seconds, but it seemed like a lifetime. I feared the boat would break loose and drag me by the leg, drowning me as it floated downstream. I howled for help, hoping someone had a knife to cut me loose. The river's power was dragging me under. On Good Friday, none-the-less.

"Great," I thought, "What a day to die."

Then I got the chain lose. I broke free and began to rush downstream. Exhaustion overwhelmed me and I couldn't stop from being swept into another, smaller tree rootball. As I floundered and took in a mouthful of water, I felt an arm grab my bicep and pull.

One of the two Good Samaritans had dragged me out of the current. I scrambled onto the sandy shore and hit my knees, shivering from the fear, the cold and the fatigue.

The two men began trying to break the boat free. The motor had been lodged into the tree, anchoring it to the snag. The roots loosened – the men were trying to avoid being pinned underwater by the boat, too. The current and the pushing finally dislodged the stricken boat, sending it downstream. One of the guys grabbed the same chain that had wrapped around my ankle (which is still sore and swollen). I took it from him and began to wrestle with the boat. Jim and the other men joined me as we played a desperate game of tug-of-war.

That's when two more guardian angels arrived on the scene.

Sonny and Bud, friends of Jim (and now my friends), had been fishing upstream and came cruising by. To quote Bud, "We came by and I saw the boat, but I had no idea it was you." They stopped to help and joined us as we wrestled the boat to the other side of the sandbar. It took five of us, but we managed to break the suction and flip it over. And that's when we began to bail the water out. Sonny had a can in his boat. I used the motor cover from Jim's boat. Bud grabbed the motor cover off of Sonny's boat.

The water-logged Phoenix, stricken boat rose again.

While the two guys knew how to get the water out of the

engine, they lacked the tools to do so. So Sonny took my son and me back to the truck (good thing I saved the keys) so we could get Jim's toolbox into the boat.

My son and I stayed behind to dry out and warm up. Sonny went back to the sandbar with the tools.

They had managed to get the motor running again briefly, but the gas was corrupted with water. The engine stalled. Two hours later, Sonny returned to the boat drop, pulling Jim and Bud.

We had lost a few things (my son's hat and a borrowed jacket, mats in the boat, straps for the boat trailer) but all in all, the whole day turned out to become a giant miracle. Angels looked over us every step of the way.

Since the motor was dead, we had to winch the salvaged boat onto the drive-on trailer by hand. Once we pulled the boat out of the water, it was over. And we were safe.

I think Jim and I replayed the events over and over that evening. Jim was very calm during the crisis. I was thankful he and I were able to keep my son out of harm's way (my son was calm, too). A freakish accident had marred a fantastic morning of fishing. But we kept thinking of all the scenarios of how things could have gone tragically wrong. That night, I apologized to my son. He held both hands by his head and then ran them down his body to his toes. And then he looked me in the eyes said something that shows why the boy is nothing short of brilliant: "Dad. It's OK. I'm here."

He's here. Thanks to luck and quick action, he's here. Thanks to two guardian angels' protection, he's here. I'm here. Jim's here. It took a nine-year-old's wisdom to remind me of that. It's not what might have happened; it's what happened.

We were blessed nearly every step of the way.

I can tell you this: When we are near water, my family members will wear their life jackets. I owe two men for my life. And I can tell you this much: My son and I got a hell of a story to tell.

He wrote this poem about his day:

Today we went out of town,
On the River our ship went down.
Two men saved our lives,

They helped gather our supplies.
There was a man named Sonny
And he was very funny.
And when it ended,
I love the time we spended.

As you can see, he sees it as an adventure. And we both learned a very valuable lesson: What doesn't kill you gives you a story to tell.

Man's Best Friend

Lightning danced between the thunderheads as dusk fell across the cotton fields. "Looks like a storm coming in from the east, ol' boy." Farmer Jack Fransconi secured his green tractor in the rusty-roofed, red barn as he talked to his little brown dog.

The dog, a terrier named Harvey, scratched behind his ear and watched the sky with a wary eye. Not a big fan of storms, the dog noticed that the clouds rolled across the Mississippi Delta in an odd way. "They look artificial," he thought. "Not of this world."

Little Harvey was more right than he knew.

A cylindrical space craft was hiding behind the clouds. It was the scout ship for a massive alien invasion force. Like Independence Day, War of the Worlds and a thousand other stories about alien invaders, these aliens weren't visiting in peace. They were looking for a new home. And ground zero for their attack would be a small, dried-up town in the Mississippi Delta.

Quint, Mississippi, had a population of 150 humans and 78 dogs. There were dogs of all sizes and breeds. Big dogs. Little dogs. Hunting dogs and stray dogs. The town had 36 buildings, a town square, four churches and a small gas station on the main road. The scout ship landed behind the gas station, not far from the Fransconi farm. When the ship touched down, four massive figures emerged and walked onto a ramp.

The speeding pickup truck holding the farmer and the dog didn't see the aliens until it was too late.

If the workers in the gas station hadn't had the radio cranked, they would have heard the impact. The truck struck the fourth alien, killing him. The other three pulled their guns from their suits and fired, halting the Chevrolet in its tracks.

"Get out," the lead alien commanded. The farmer, who was on the verge of a heart attack, and the small dog fell out of the cabin. A flash of light revealed the oak trees and brush. The farmer lay unconscious next to the truck. "Take him to the ship," the lead alien commanded. Harvey growled. "Easy, boy. We're one of your kind." The lead alien took off his mask, revealing a canine head. "We're here to conquer this planet for all dogs."

Harvey looked up at the tall alien and said, "You're not my kind. I wouldn't have hurt the farmer." The alien grinned and said, "Tell your friends we are here. We are here to liberate dogs from humans. We're from the fourth planet from what you call the dog star."

Harvey ran away. He wanted to help the farmer but he knew he couldn't do anything about it right now. He ran toward Quint barking his head off. Like Paul Revere, he was warning the world. "The aliens are coming! The aliens are coming!" The world, however, was not listening.

By the time Harvey made it into downtown, he saw that all the humans had been rounded up and put into a pen in the town square. Dogs barked nervously as they ran around the chain link fence. The three aliens carried the farmer's unconscious body onto the grass and threw him down. He groggily started to move.

The dogs all gathered around the aliens, growling. Rex, the police dog, ran at the second alien, wanting to rip him to shreds. The third alien pulled his pistol out and shot Rex, stopping him in his tracks. The lead alien stepped on the limp German Shepherd. "You can do this one of two ways. I would recommend you choose peacefully."

The dogs slumped. They had to rescue their humans but they didn't know how.

Dottie, the town Dalamatian, looked at Rex's body and said, "If you can't beat them, join them. And when you join them, find their weakness. We have to stop these guys somehow. We have to find someone who can get aboard their ship. But who?"

Harvey stepped forward. "I will. I know where their ship is." He stopped for a moment and scratched behind his ear. "#$%# fleas!" The other dogs nodded. They agreed 100 percent. In a way, the aliens were as bad of parasites as their arch enemies the fleas.

Later that night, the aliens were searching trailer to trailer, looked for any remaining humans. Harvey ran back through the darkness to the Fransconi farm. The alien craft was illuminated and abandoned. Harvey ran up the ramp and into the hold. What he saw disgusted him (and he was a dog).

Hanging from the ceiling was a stripped cow. Bones and meat lay heaped on the ground. Pools of blood were everywhere. He realized that these alien dogs had a taste for blood. And he knew what the aliens would eat when they invaded. Time was short. His master was about to become lunch.

He scratched his ear again. And then he began looking around.

Nothing made sense. The aliens spoke dog, but the dogs didn't read alien. He flipped a few knobs and tried to see if he could sabotage the ship. No luck. He scratched one more time. Then he looked out the window. The aliens were coming — he had to get off the ship.

He ran down the ramp and into the darkness. The other dogs would be disappointed. As he ran toward the town, he realized that he had failed.

The next morning, the dogs approached the alien ship quietly. There was no sign of movement on it as they snuck around to the ramp. Harvey quietly crawled up the ramp. Still nothing. He looked into the room where he had seen the cow and saw the three aliens lying on the floor. All seemed to be unconscious. Harvey walked up to them and was shocked.

They were dead.

He called out to the other dogs and they came aboard the ship. Ralphie the Lab looked at the bodies closely. "They have hundreds of red welts on them." Sadie the Jack Russell, also examining the invaders, said what they all were thinking, "Fleas. They've been killed by fleas." All the dogs started barking and laughing. Their worst enemy had become their best friend.

When they got back into town square, Frank the Great Dane pushed open the gate. The residents of Quint found their dog and cheered their freedom. And high above their heads, the alien invasion fleet tucked tail and headed home.

It was on that fall day in a small Mississippi Delta town that a motley group of dogs truly became man's best friend.

A Mother's Day Shopping Guide.

I was trying to think of what the boys and I could get Amy for Mother's Day. Here are a few things that rattled from my brain:

- A George Foreman Grill.
- A cup of Nightcrawlers and a Zebco 202.
- A book of McDonaldland Gift Certificates.
- Dipping Dots — the Ice Cream of the Future.
- An ant farm.
- Sea Monkeys
- A Mr. Microphone.
- A gift card to my favorite restaurant.
- A Soccer ball
- An Apple Watch.

Hmmm. No, I don't think she would appreciate any of those. Especially anything that could be considered an "appliance."

Maybe I'll get her something she likes wrapped in a big red bow called appreciation. And maybe an Apple Watch with my name on it.

A Dog's Tail

A blue deep-v fishing boat emerged from the mist and quietly glided up to the dock. Water lapped gently against the shore, making the only sound for miles. An elderly woman with a white robe, orange ski belt and impish smile tied a yellow rope to the post. An old dog wagged his tail and waited patiently.

"Why, hello there, old friend. It's good to see you again."

The dog, with gray around his muzzle, barked once and wagged his tail harder. Dogs can see much more than people.

The lady clumsily got out of the boat, knocking her tackle box askew. "Oh, drat. Stripers are running this morning. Been using a spoon. Of course, Heaven is catch and release."

She had been dead for five years, but to her it seemed like she had been fishing for only an hour.

That particular dock along the Tennessee River was a portal between two worlds. Locals had said that this spot, so beautiful and idyllic, seemed like Heaven. Little did they know, they were almost right.

"Is he in trouble again?"

The dog barked. But this time his tail wasn't wagging.

She sighed. She had watched over her grandson since he was just a child. He was a good boy, a talented boy. But his heart wasn't in the right place. He was full of anger. The young man held onto a grudge with a death grip.

"Well, then, I guess it is up to us to save him." She picked up her old dog, causing him to glow slightly. "We have work to do." The two of them headed off to save a soul.

Patrick Karns was a talented man with an eye for business and the uncanny ability to step on people on his way to the top. At the age of 30, he had started a computer software company. He had truly achieved the American Dream and then proceeded to turn into a nightmare. His wife hated him. His kids were indifferent. People at work feared him. Now, at the age of 47, he was like an EF-5 tornado: Patrick left nothing but destruction in his path. He had put the word suck in success.

He sat alone, drinking a glass of very expensive wine, thinking lovingly of the most important person in the world: Himself.

The little dog barked at the back door.

"What do you want?"

The dog growled. "Shhh, the grandmother said. Honey catches more flies than vinegar."

The dog barked again, this time with a smile and a tail-wag.

"OK, OK." Patrick got up and walked over to the door. He reached down to smack the dog and when he touched the dog's head, he clutched his heart. Pain shot up his arm. But it wasn't a heart attack. It was something else. Something more powerful.

The grandmother held the dog by the tail and watched as her grandson experienced the full fury of Hell. Demons and fire consumed his soul. Every cell of his body felt nothing but anger and pain. He screamed as his hand was stuck to the little dog. She reached and grabbed her grandson's hand and pulled him back from the brink. Then she showed him a glimpse of paradise. The small dog felt a pleasant warmth surge through his little body. It was a love indescribable in human terms. It was easy for a dog, though. Kindness. Service to others. Love.

For a brief moment, Patrick saw his grandmother standing there, smiling and holding her little dog. And then she faded away.

"What was that?!?" he said to his dog. The little dog just barked and wagged his tail. He felt the tingle in his hand where he had touched the dog's head. It was a strange warmth that began to spread up his arm into his soul.

— — — — — — — —

Six months later, the small boat sailed back to the dock. The little dog once again waited patiently. "Why hello there!" a voice called out of thc mist.

The dog barked and wagged his tail.

"Yes, the fish are biting. They always bite in Heaven. How's our boy?"

The dog barked again and wagged his tail vigorously.

They walked back up the hill to the cabin and the grandmother was pleased at what she saw. Her grandson was a different man.

The family members sat together and were playing a game. The smartphones were in another room as they laughed and played. He was off from work for a week to take time to start a new charity and had taken some time out of his schedule for family night. He still was a powerful businessman, but like

Ebenezer Scrooge on Christmas Day, he now took an interest in the lives of his employees. He had empowered them and in the process changed their lives for the better, too. His wife looked over at him lovingly. Six months of counseling had provided some major breakthroughs in their marriage. Patrick Karns believed that the true secret of success was to have a servant's heart.

The little dog barked at the door.

Patrick got up and opened the door. "Hey, pal!" he said lovingly as the dog stood at the door. He credited the dog with changing his life.

As he reached down to pet the dog, he thought he saw his grandmother again. "Nah," he said, as he went back to the game. The dog ran back out into the yard.

The grandmother and the dog went back to the dock. As she began to untie the boat, she beckoned to the pup. "Want to go fishing with me?" The dog barked, wagged his tail and leapt into the boat.

She said, "Hold on. We're going to catch a boatful today."

And on a beautiful Tennessee evening, an old lady and a dog sailed gently into the mist.

HOW TORNADOES WERE DESCRIBED BEFORE FREIGHT TRAINS
IT SOUNDED LIKE A FLATULENT BUFFALO!
PRESS

The Waterbug

I learned several things in college: My Social Security number, how to draw editorial cartoons and the joy of a Saturday afternoon football game. But it's funny, the most important lessons were the quiet ones that were taught in odd moments in unexpected places. And many of those lessons were ones that I didn't appreciate until years later. Like today.

My oldest son was working on an English paper recently and my mind went back to the 500-word, five-paragraph essays I had to write in my early University of Tennessee English classes. I didn't consider myself a good writer back then (and probably wasn't), but I got good grades. I figured out the drill and learned how to tell a decent enough story in a properly structured way.

My sophomore year, my English class was over "The Hill" in one of the engineering buildings. I don't remember much about the class or even the teaching assistant's name, to be honest, but I do know my friend Julia Gibson Hammer was in the class with me. (Julia, I include you in this tale because you might remember the prof's name).

I settled in for several weeks of more 500-word essays.

Until one day the professor (short, fairly heavyset, thinning hair) began a different lecture. He began talking about how we need to live our lives in the moment. How we should just engage and live deeply – that we should not be like Gerridaes (water striders or water bugs) and skim across the surface of our lives.

I sat in that Engineering classroom, listening to an English teaching assistant tell me one of the most important lessons of my life. And it went completely over my head.

Until today. This evening, I'm saddened by the sudden death of someone I liked and respected. I continue to mourn a loved one who is in the early stages of dementia. Thursday, I watched my son get wheeled into surgery. And earlier that morning, I nearly tore my fingers off my drawing hand.

I am feeling very, very mortal. And tired.

And then I thought of the Gerridae. I thought of how much life I've wasted just skimming. Maybe it is time to go deeper in the water. Maybe it is time to appreciate the remarkable gift of life a little bit more.

I raise a toast to that unnamed teaching assistant. You, my

friend, were wise before my ability to realize it. And I raise a toast to the Gerridae. While you skim, I'll start to live.

The Devil and Tom Blake

The dark shadow of fear threw him into darkness. As Tom Blake sat at his desk, he felt himself gasp for air. And he felt cold. Very cold. Not a terribly religious man, Tom nevertheless knew the Devil when he met him. And that is exactly who had brought this fear. Well, the Devil and a corporate vice president. And his dad's cancer. And....

The list was longer than Tom could process at one time. A tree had fallen on his house the night before during the storm and he could feel his bloodshot eyes trying to focus. And then there was his wife. And his kids. And...

No one was happy in Tom's life. At the top of that list was Tom.

Tom gripped his coffee cup like it was a life preserver because he definitely was a drowning man. Pity washed over him like a crashing wave, sending him reeling. His soul tumbled and he once again tried to gasp. A pain hit his chest, sending him out of his chair and onto the office floor.

"You OK?" Carol, his assistant, rushed over to pull Tom off the floor.

Tom, embarrassed, sat back in his chair and apologized meekly, "Um, yeah."

Reflux. His body was even mad at him. Fear was ripping him physically apart. The Devil grinned. He'd soon have another soul.

"Good morning, Mr. Blake." It was Barry, the man who came by every morning to empty the trash. "Blessed day we're having today, isn't it?"

Tom scoffed. How could a man who emptied the trash be having a good day? Heck, the man should be more disgruntled than he was.

"What's so good about it?" Tom spewed his venom.

But Barry wasn't buying it.

"We're above the dirt, Mr. Blake."

"You can call me Tom, Barry. You're my elder after all."

Barry laughed, "Age isn't a number. It's what is between here." He pointed to the space between his ears, "Hey, you got a minute?"

Tom didn't, but he said, "Sure."

Barry led him to the window.

"See all those people?"

Both men stared at all the people on the sidewalk below. It was lunchtime and the streets looked like someone had kicked over a fire ant nest.

"You know how many of them are problem-free?"

Tom shrugged his shoulders, "I dunno."

"None of them," Barry said, "In fact, the only people who have no problems are dead."

Tom thought they were the lucky ones.

"No," Barry said while almost reading his mind. "You are the lucky one. Fear has knocked on your door and brought you opportunity. But you have to stand up to it, first. Show courage."

Tom looked out at the people below. Cancer. Financial problems. Disease. Depression. Fear. It was all down there. But they kept going. They kept moving. They stood up to the Devil.

Barry emptied another garbage can. Just like he had Tom's mind.

"You know, the only person who loves a pity party is the person who is throwing it."

Tom smiled as Barry walked away. There seemed to be a glow coming from the old man, but he couldn't figure out why.

Six months later, Tom's life had changed radically. He had been laid off. His father had died of cancer. His wife and he had separated. But Tom didn't lie down. He kept pushing through the pain. Eventually he got a better job. And he and his wife reconciled. They fixed the foundation of their marriage and joy rendered their household. Tom made time to spend with his kids. He found joy in unexpected places. In return, more joy came his way. Fear continued to visit him, but Tom no longer felt afraid. He faced it head on and it had changed his life forever.

He couldn't help but think of Barry. How could have a simple man have changed his path so drastically? As he threw the football to his son, he laughed. "Sometimes, son, angels show up to empty your trash."

Looking for Christmas

I went looking for Christmas yesterday. In all the hustle and bustle, stress, change and challenges, I haven't been able to find it this year. So I went on a quest to find it.

I didn't find it at the Jackson airport. But I did see the Lord's handiwork somewhere over eastern Mississippi as the sun broke over the horizon. The plane dipped into the clouds, making us feel like we were doing a low-level trench run through mountain peaks. The normally white, puffy nimbus clouds were painted orange to celebrate a new day.

A day I knew would be emotional.

But Christmas wasn't on my Delta flight. I enjoyed my delicious Delta cookie and prepared myself for the soulless joy that is Hartsfield-Jackson airport. Maybe Christmas would be there.

Nope. It wasn't. But I did see one of the stars of one of my favorite shows. And he did play Jesus once in a movie — so that's kind of close. I rented a car and headed out onto Atlanta's interstates.

Trust me, there is no Christmas spirit on I-285.

I pulled up to my parent's home — a house where they have lived for nearly all my whole life. I looked in the backyard where I played as a child. I closed my eyes and all my childhood dogs came running to the fence to greet me. Then as soon as my eyes opened, their ghosts were gone.

I opened the backdoor and walked in — you never have to knock at your mama's house, you know — and was greeted by my dad. That he knew me was a special gift. My mom came out, too. She looked pretty in her reddish sweater. I hugged them and tried to lock that memory into my mind. But I'm learning that memories aren't to be taken for granted. They can be stolen as easily as the Grinch steals a Whoville Roast Beast.

We went to my dad's doctor's appointment and then out to eat. Christmas carols played quietly in the restaurant. But Christmas wasn't there for me. My mind was filled with worry. My search continued.

The afternoon flew faster than the plane I needed to catch and I had to say goodbye to my parents. I'll see them in a few days — but as days go by, I realize what a precious commodity time really is. "A few days" might as well be a lifetime. I watched them as I pulled away — I know that I'll soon be watching my own children pull away. I'm not prepared for that. I'm not sure my parents ever have gotten used to it, either.

A friend from high school called and said a bunch of them had formed a men's prayer group and they were wrapping gifts for needy kids. It was on my way to the airport, so I stopped in for 15-minutes and saw many of my childhood friends. They've all grown into good, good men. I don't what it was about my high school, but we turned out OK.

I headed back south through downtown Atlanta and on to the airport. I dropped off my car, rushed through security and ate some delicious airport food. My flight was crammed tight and I watched quietly as dozens of people, each with his or her own stories to tell, entered my life for our shared flight. Our plane pushed back from the gate and its engines roared to life (I was in the back by the engines — so they REALLY roared). I suspended my search for Christmas as the plane once again defied gravity.

Somewhere over Alabama, I mentally replayed my day. First, I thought about the sunrise on the morning's flight. Then I remembered my dad's smile when I told him about my son's Scouting achievements. I marveled at the beauty of the skyscrapers in downtown Atlanta. My heart warmed from the memories of my childhood. I thought of my old friends not just preaching their faith but actually living it. I saw kind acts in an airport that is too busy for kindness. I felt love for my parents. I was grateful I had survived Atlanta's rush hour. I found good in a sea of bad.

And as the Delta flight touched down in Jackson, Mississippi, I felt something I have not felt in a long, long time.

I felt peace.

I had found Christmas after all.

Gibson's Gift

A father and son sat bathed in the glow of a large, fake Christmas tree. Its white lights bathed them quietly in its warmth. The little boy broke the silence.

"You know that if you do the math, there's no way Santa can visit EVERY house around the world in 24 hours."

Gibson looked at his son Davis and shook his head. The kid was six going on 46.

"There are a lot of naughty kids, Davis. It cuts Santa's workload considerably."

Davis bought his dad's explanation and went back to playing ZombieAttack on his dad's phone.

But Gibson knew that his son probably would Google it later tonight. The Internet had sped up the death of innocence. His son could now be exposed to things he never knew about until he had joined the Navy. His kid could learn in three simple keystrokes what it took him three cruises on the U.S.S. Nimitz to learn.

Then his son dropped the big one:

"Is Santa real?"

Gibson remembered when he had asked his father that question. Of course, Gibson had been 16, not six.

"Do you want him to be real?" Gibson asked in his best lawyerly dodge.

"Yeah."

"Then he's real. If you believe, you'll receive."

Davis sat silently, trying to wrap his mind around his father's answer. He wanted to believe in Santa and didn't care what Jenny Franklin said.

Silence quickly returned and the father and son stared at the tree. Gibson remembered lying on his parent's living room couch and staring at their Scotch pine tree. It had red bulbs that burned as hot as the sun. How the house had not burned down was nothing short of a Christmas Miracle. Back then, it took forever for Christmas to arrive. But Christmas vacation had lasted much longer then. Now he worked all the time. And that made time speed by as fast as Santa's reindeer. College had been when he noticed time starting to fly. Now it was supersonic.

Davis grabbed a handful of sand dabs and drank some milk.

Powered sugar ringed his mouth. Eating sand dab cookies was a Christmas tradition passed along from his grandparents.

Gibson's grandparents. Gibson remembered waiting for them to arrive from Texas. He'd fall asleep on the den floor, hoping that would cause time to speed up so they'd get there a little bit quicker.

Time did speed up. And then it ran out.

"Dad, what do you want from Santa?"

"Socks from my grandparents, hand delivered."

Davis patted his dad's back. "Santa's good. But I'm not sure he's that good. Hey, you know that Rudolph's on TV. Let's go watch together. I hear Hermie wants to be a dentist and Bumbles bounce."

Rudolph. At least some things never changed.

Gibson picked his son up and carried him into the family room to watch TV. As they watched the Rankin Bass classic, time ground to a halt.

And for Gibson, that was the finest Christmas gift of all.

IT'S ALL HOW YOU LOOK AT THINGS.
NOT ANOTHER HILL to CLIMB.
I BET the VIEW IS AWESOME!

Christmas Movies and Shows That Should Never Be Remade.

- *The Grinch Who Stole Christmas* (my proof – love the cartoon, hate the movie).
- *Rudolph the Red Nosed Reindeer* (TV Show)
- *Frosty the Snowman*
- *It's a Wonderful Life*
- *A Charlie Brown Christmas*
- *A Christmas Story*
- *Christmas Vacation*
- *Elf*
- *Santa Claus Is Coming to Town*
- *Miracle on 34th Street* (Natalie Wood version)
- *Die Hard* (I really don't think it is technically a Christmas movie, but hey, it has a tree in it and takes place at Christmas)

Russell Rudolph's Christmas

"You look handsome."

Rusty Randolph's mother used spit to try to tame his cowlick.

The seven-year-old's wild blonde hair shot toward the cold, night sky.

"C'mon MOM!" Rusty protested. It was really more than having spit used as hair product that bothered him. It was Christmas Eve and he was in the worst place possible for a kid. He was in church. Minutes seemed like hours. Hours, well, it was just taking too darn long. His mom said they were there for the true meaning of Christmas. Rusty had yet to see Santa Claus.

Finally, a priest walked up to the front of the church and began to speak. To Rusty, he sounded like Charlie Brown's parents. "Waa Waa Waa Waa." But then his words came through remarkably clear, "It is better to give than receive."

"What?" It was a message that was totally lost on a seven-year-old boy.

As they finally walked out of the cathedral, Rusty looked up at the night sky. There, near the moon, was a blinking red light.

"RUDOLPH! MOM, WE HAVE TO GO HOME NOW! THERE'S RUDOLPH!!" The passengers on the Boeing 727 above were oblivious to the little boy and his dreams of presents.

Forty years later.

"DAD! Did you fix my lunch?" Russell Randolph looked around the kitchen for his oldest son's brown paper lunch sack.

"I think so."

Getting the kids out of the house in the morning was like invading France on a daily basis. D-Day was every day. And this morning they were fighting a losing battle.

"I got my shoes on." Russell looked down at his seven-year-old. The kid had put his shoes on the wrong feet.

"Jesus Chr...." Russell caught himself. He knew his blood pressure must be in the Stratosphere and he didn't want to tempt fate and a heart attack by using Jesus' name in vain. He reached over and flipped on the kitchen TV. War. Check. Murder. Check. Racial strife. Check. Plane Crash. Check. Terrorism. Check. Extreme weather. Check.

Russell felt the acid rising in his throat.

In five minutes he had gotten a quick reminder what a screwed up world his kids were inheriting. Now he knew he'd have a heart attack.

"You seen my keys?" Russell's wife Becky screamed from the garage.

Becky taught at the local elementary school and was, once again, late.

"They are in your car."

"Oh. Bye!"

Between their jobs and schlepping the kids around, he couldn't remember the last time he and Becky had had a conversation other than about the kids or running the household.

"Oh, did you pay the water bill?" she yelled from the running SUV.

Russell felt a wave of stupid wash over him. "DAMMIT," he yelled. His kids stopped and looked at him.

Dad NEVER cussed.

"Let me guess, yet another thing you forgot," Becky scolded him. Sometimes it was like she had four kids, not three. Russell slinked back into the kitchen, frustrated and defeated. Russell's mind had been slipping. Like the beach during a hurricane, life's woes and problems had surged over his brain, leaving him mentally flooded. "

Um. I'll get to it." He looked over at the Christmas tree that was in living room. He then looked at the credit card bills on the counter.

He hated Christmas.

The fuss. The expense. The stress. Even putting up the tree was a pain in the butt. Peace on Earth, good will to man was such a crock of bull. He was over Christmas. He flipped off the TV.

The little boy from 40 years ago was no more.

It was a cold, dreary December day. Russell backed out of this driveway, noted the piles of leaves and felt his chest tighten again. He headed out of the neighborhood and tried to think of everything he had to do. It was the last day of work before Christmas vacation and he was slammed. There was going to be another round of layoffs and he didn't know if he'd survive. Everyone in the office was on edge and there wasn't much Joy to the World at work either.

He spent the next ten hours in a cubicle sitting next to fear. He felt much older than his 47 years.

On the way home, Russell listened to the talk radio host. He normally loved the guy — who loved to give the president hell. Russell loved to get worked up on the way home every day. But Russell noticed something for the first time tonight. The man was trying to scare him. Fear was pouring out of the radio. And Russell felt very afraid. So he put on his blinker and took a sudden left. He drove across town to the cathedral where his mother had dragged him 40 years earlier.

The car stopped in front of it and he trudged through the rain to the steps. He stopped and refused to go in. So he just sat there. Like Moses on the edge of the Promised Land, he looked at the entrance and knew he couldn't enter.

He sat in the dark as cold rain poured down on his head. Darkness wrapped his body and soul — all except the faint, multicolored light from the stained glass. And if you had looked closed enough, you'd have noticed that rain wasn't the only water trickling down his face.

"You'll catch pneumonia out here, son."

The voice sounded familiar. Russell snapped out of his pity party and looked around. His eyes could barely make out a figure walking out of the shadows holding an umbrella.

"Since you don't want to come in, I thought I'd come to you."

Russell looked at the older man's face. A moment of recognition jolted him. It was the priest from his childhood.

"Christmas getting you down?"

Russell nodded. "Yes, sir. And the rest of life. I can't see anything good about the world."

The priest laughed. "Son, if you can't see good in the world, be the good in the world."

Russell was a lousy poker player. He glared at the father with a look of confusion.

"You're almost as thick as you were when you were seven."

Russell was shocked the priest remembered him. "Oh yes, I remember you. You had that cowlick that your mother was always trying to tame with spit."

Russell sat up straight. He looked at the priest and started to talk. "But we live in a broken world…"

The priest cut him off. "Rusty, the world is the world. Like a stone hitting a still pond, you have a way to change it. You can change it with your actions. Those actions can be good. They can be bad. Or they can be nothing at all. You have the power but it starts here," the priest pointed at his heart, "here," then his brain, "but most importantly here," he pointed toward heaven.

Russell looked up at the sky. The rain had stopped and the clouds began to part. A full moon and stars peeked from behind the clouds.

"Russell, be the good in people's lives. Give them a Christmas present they'll never forget. Like I tried to tell you so many years ago, "It's better to give than to receive."

The priest slowly got up and started to walk back toward the darkness.

"Merry Christmas, Rusty."

Russell smiled and said, "And to you, father."

He sat for 15 more minutes and then stood up and walked into the cathedral. On a side hall, near the bathroom was a framed photo of his priest.

In memory of Father Joseph Hurley, 1935-1979

May he rest in peace.

Russell's jaw dropped. He stood there, stunned and staring at the man's wizened face. He then looked around. The building was empty. No one was around.

Rusty Randolph realized he had been given one of the greatest Christmas gifts of all.

Starting a Fire

Frost crunched under the two figures' feet as they walked quietly through the frozen Mississippi woods. Record cold blanketed the land as the grandfather felt how cold his grandson's hands were. They needed to build a fire to stay warm. And they needed to do it now.

A cold front had blown through earlier in the week, leaving five inches of rain and Arctic air behind. The ground was frozen and the wood was wet. Building a fire would be difficult at best. The grandfather smiled and thought of Jack London's *To Build a Fire*. That book made him cold even in August.

His grandson shivered and then squeaked, "Papa James, I'm cold." Like the man in the book, the grandfather realized he had to succeed. Just hopefully with better results.

"I know you are cold Danny. We'll have a fire going in no time."

The little boy watched as his grandfather gathered the wood and believed him. The old man found some dryish leaves and brought them over, too. He fumbled in his pocket for a box of matches. They had the supplies. They had the desire. They had the need. Now it was up to his grandfather's know-how. And his persistence.

The old man stacked the wood carefully and made it easy for oxygen to get into the fire. "Fire needs fuel and oxygen," he told the boy. "Otherwise it will smother. That's why you stop, drop and roll. You try to cut off the fire's oxygen."

The little boy was half listening. His hands were bitterly cold and hurt.

Each attempt at lighting the fire failed. The wood was wet. The leaves wouldn't catch. But the grandfather didn't quit. And he didn't keep trying the same things. He adjusted his plan. He found some dry paper in his backpack and lit it. Eventually the wood ignited. And soon, the two were enjoying a toasty, blazing fire.

"Remember this, boy," the grandfather said as he held his shivering grandson tight. "Persistence is the secret ingredient of life. If we had quit, we'd be really, really cold. But we didn't. And now we're enjoying the warmth of a fire. Sometimes a fire won't come easy. You have to keep trying new things and never stop until you get it to light."

The lesson was lost on the little boy – until 35 years later.

Daniel sat in his office of his small business with his head in his hands. The numbers didn't look good.

In a small gift shop in a suburb of Jackson, Mississippi, Daniel looked at the picture of his grandfather he kept on his office desk. What would the old man do in this situation?

Daniel had been laid off from his job in 2010. He had courageously taken the family savings and opened a small, unique gift shop that offered the best items of Mississippi. While his rent was high, the shopping center received great traffic. Until the outlet mall opened and sucked customers away like a black hole.

His business had gone cold. He needed to build a fire. And the wood was wet.

He thought of that night in the woods. He imagined his grandfather standing there calmly changing strategies. He had a goal and was going to achieve it – he had to achieve it. He thought of his grandfather's persistence.

He looked around. He had been trying to do things the way he had done them the previous three years. Daniel sat down with a piece of paper and thought of ways he could get his business moving again, too. He Googled ideas and brainstormed. Like his grandfather flicking matches, he kept throwing new ideas out there until a fire started.

He changed his marketing strategy. He redesigned the floor plan of his store to make it more inviting. He used social media more and created a popular twitter account that offered free advice and personified his business. He told stories about each piece of merchandise in his store. He created a strong online storefront and began shipping unique Mississippi gifts worldwide. He became a storyteller and told his store's story. He found his strengths – his dry wood, so to speak – and he lit them.

Within six months, his store was enjoying record profits.

Daniel looked out at the customers in his shop and thought of his grandfather. He was thankful the old man had taught him not to quit when things were tough. Some grandparents give their grandkids toys and cash. Papa James had given him the gift of persistence during tough times. He tried new things instead of making excuses. And it was one of the most precious gifts of all.

Ten Things I Learned from Retail

1. You hustle. And then you hustle some more.
2. If you take a break, you miss a sale.
3. It's all about engagement. You have to find out what the customer needs and serve that need.
4. Talking to the customer is your greatest source of marketing information.
5. You can't fall in love with your product. If it doesn't sell, find something that does.
6. ABN: Always Be Nice. A smile, eye contact and a friendly hello go a long way in a crazy world.
7. You have to create an experience for customers. They can buy somewhere else — and probably for cheaper.
8. Wear comfortable shoes. Concrete is not your friend.
9. There is no guaranteed check at the end of the day. You have to go out and hunt to bring home your supper.
10. It's a great way to meet new friends.

Roses are red,
Violets are blue.
Since you forgot
Valentine's Day
It's the couch
for you...
TO MY
IDIOT
HUSBAND

The Dead Oak in Winter

Jack and June Barnhill's marriage stood like a dead oak in winter. From the outside, it looked strong and mighty. But on the inside, it was brittle, twisted and rotten. After 50 years of marriage, they sat across from each other in their home's den, trying not to breathe the same air. They had long passed "for better" in their relationship. Now they were smack in the middle of "for worse."

Sarcasm replaced kindness; Angry glares stood in for loving looks.

"You can leave me, you know."

"But that would bring you happiness. I want to stay right here and make you completely miserable."

"Congratulations. You're doing a darn good job."

"You know, this Ex-Lax commercial could be a short film about your life."

"And the Preparation H one about yours."

"Well, I did marry a pain in the..."

The cat, tired of the constant bickering, gave up and went into the other room. Even the Grinch would have had enough of their bitterness.

Their two children, tired of being put in the middle of their parents' feuds, moved as far away as from them as they possible could. Jack, Jr., an engineer for Boeing, lived in Everett, Washington. Jennifer, an internal medicine doctor, lived in Maine.

They only came home once a year. If that often.

"Well, if you will excuse me, I have to clean the kitchen. I don't want you to touch the water. You'll melt."

"Sit down, martyr. If you did any work around here, the roof would collapse."

June, 75, got out of her plaid recliner and shuffled toward the kitchen. What happened next would change their lives forever.

She entered the kitchen and collapsed. Jack heard grizzly smack as her head hit the tile floor.

"OK, Drama Queen. You can come back now."

But there was no response.

"June? June?!? JUNE!"

Jack leapt to the kitchen and saw her body lying on the tile floor. A small circle of crimson began to grow from the gaping wound on her forehead.

Jack screamed, "OMIGOD! HELP!" He pulled the phone from his pocket and dialed 911. "My wife is unconscious at 98 Windchime Ct. She fell and is bleeding! Hurry!!

It was the first time since Vietnam that he was truly afraid.

"Hold on, June. Hold on," he cried as he tried to stop the bleeding.

Bitterness had been replaced by something even more cold — fear.

The next day later, Jack Jr. and Jennifer arrived from the airport. They walked into the hospital room and found their parents together. Their mother was on the bed unconscious; their father with his head lying across her. The children stood in the doorway, watching with awe as their father slowly stroked their mom's unwashed gray hair. He then raised his head and whispered loudly into her ear.

"I'm sorry for all the times I pissed you off — well, most of them. I'm sorry for all the cold nights. I'm sorry that we lost our way. If you come back to me, I'll change. I can't live life without your insults. Life without your cranky voice would be torture. The house would be too quiet. My heart would be too empty. I had forgotten how much I loved you until now."

He broke down and began to openly sob.

As he did, a single tear trickled down the old woman's face.

In that Mississippi hospital room, old wounds were healed. A marriage, cold and bitter, still had a little life left in it after all. And the dead oak in winter sprang back to life.

The Sign

As the University of Tennessee's football team members walk out of their locker room and onto the field, there is a sign above the door that each team member touches.

It reads: "I will give my all for Tennessee today."

I love that. In fact, I like it so well, I am going to modify it ever so slightly and hang it on our door out to the garage.

Our sign will read, "I will give my all for this family today."

Because that's what it is all about. We either succeed as a family or we fail as one. Everything I do is for Amy and my boys. And remembering that larger purpose is healthy.

The Matchmaker

The Angel of Death doesn't actually do her own killing. She hires hit men, mercenaries if you will, to do her dirty work. These are people who'll trade a little bit of their souls for more time on this Earth. Today's killer was chosen to take out Fredrick Simms II, an investment banker and all-around jerk. Aged 45, Fredrick was on his second divorce and had screwed over more people than WorldCom and Enron combined. The Angel of Death admired his ruthlessness. But he had to go. It was just his time.

Three-time con Barry McReady was assigned the job of eliminating Fredrick. The Angel of Death laid out the plan: Barry would meet Fredrick (who was on a business trip to New Orleans) on the corner of Conti and Bourbon streets in the French Quarter. Barry would approach Fredrick and ask for money. Then when Fredrick refused, Barry would shoot him in the stomach with a .22 snub-nosed revolver. Fredrick would bleed-out in front of total strangers and Barry would run away.

At least that is how it was supposed to happen.

But Barry had been a loser his whole life. And on the night of his biggest job ever, he messed that up, too. The gun went off, sending Fredrick to the ground. But the gunshot wound was too far to the right, making it, at best, superficial. Sure, Fredrick bled. But not enough to kill him. Barry looked down at the man he thought he had killed and ran.

But Barry didn't see the police car responding to the gunshot. The Ford Crown Victoria hit the running shooter and Barry's head hit the pavement. He was killed instantly.

Fredrick's consciousness faded as he cheated death and slipped into a coma.

The Angel of Death doesn't tolerate failure. And because of it, Barry paid with his life and soul. She looked down at Fredrick's body on the ground. To make up for the screw up, Fredrick was rewarded with a second chance. The Angel of Death wiped Barry's memory and slate clean.

Fredrick's memory would come back in bits and pieces — but only the good parts. The dark side of Fredrick Simms died that night in the French Quarter. By the time he left Charity Hospital, Fredrick was a new man who had to fit back into his old world.

It wouldn't go well.

"What's wrong with him?" one of his partners asked.

"I don't know. He seems, so, well you know, nice."

"That gunshot wound took his edge. We can't have that kind of cancer around here."

The firm of Ruthless, Ruthless and Simms soon lost one of its founding partners. Within four months, Fredrick was given a huge severance package and sent into a new life.

That night, surrounded by cardboard packing boxes, Fredrick thought of where he could move. He wanted to start a new life in a new place – place where he could start a new old life. Fredrick got on his laptop and booked a one-way flight to Mobile, Alabama.

He was going home.

Fredrick had graduated from the Mitchell College of Business at the University of South Alabama in 1991. Talented enough to go to Harvard, he did just that for grad school. He went on to earn his MBA and moved back home to make his fortune. He worked ungodly hours in a skyscraper overlooking the Mobile River shipyards. While on a weekend trip to Orange Beach, he met a young girl working in one of the souvenir shops. Her name was Stacy Duval and she had the whitest smile and tannest skin. After two weeks, they had gotten married and lived in Fredrick's small bungalow near Fairhope. If passion gave off electricity, they could have lit downtown Mobile for 50 years.

But Fredrick's dark side soon revealed itself. His ego was too big for one woman, even if she was perfect. Stacy left Fredrick and divorced him soon afterward. Fredrick left for New York. The rest is, as they say, misery.

Now a decade later, Fredrick would win her back. But proving you're not a monster is easier said than done. He went back home in search of the first love of his life.

Stacy had remarried a year after her divorce from Fredrick to Sergeant Stan Hughes, U.S. Army. They had a daughter named Julia after his first tour of duty in Afghanistan. But soon he was gone again. And again. And again. Three months into his third tour, the Angel of Death used the Taliban to take Stan from this world. Stacy was now a widow, divorcee and a single mom. She vowed on Stan's casket that she would raise their daughter well.

She watched on that muggy July morning as his casket dropped down into the ground. And her heart went into the ground with it. "I'll never love anyone again — well, other than Julia." Stacy's heart grew cold.

The Angel of Death watched all of this and for one of the first times ever, felt guilty. She would intervene once again.

Tourist traffic choked the idyllic streets of Fairhope. Summer was the busy season for Gulf Coast Tours and Clarence the driver cursed as he tried to navigate his tour bus through the glut of cars. He felt pressure in his chest. He felt weird, almost odd. Sweat beaded his forehead and pain shot up his left arm. It was his time to go.

And the Angel of Death was handling this one personally.

The driverless bus creamed through the intersection, aiming right for Stacy and Julia in the crosswalk.

But before it could hit them, a man ran from the curb and pushed them out of the way onto the ground.

The bus creamed into a building, and tipped perilously. The man who pushed Stacy and Julia out of the way then got up and ran over to the bus to help rescue the passengers. He grabbed an extinguisher and put out a small fire. Other than Clarence the bus driver, there were no other fatalities. *The Mobile Press-Register* would profile the hero in Sunday's paper. His name was Fredrick Simms. And he was just in the right place at the right time.

Stacy looked at her rescuer with complete disbelief.

"Fredrick, is that you?"

She brushed sand and gravel out of her bloody knee. Tears welled in her eyes. She then started talking to herself.

"It can't be Fredrick. He would have run the other way."

Fredrick tenderly felt the burns on his hands. He looked at his ex-wife and the little girl with her. Tears started to well in his eyes, too.

"Stacy? Stacy is that you?"

"You saved us."

"You saved me." Fredrick looked at her. "I have missed you."

Stacy felt the pain from so many years ago stab at her heart. She started to back away.

"NO! No! I am a changed man. Promise!" Fredrick stopped

and raised his shirt. A grotesque scar showed where the bullet had killed evil Fredrick.

Stacy looked at the red scar and said, "You need to get your hands looked at."

Fredrick looked at them. They were bright red and burned. But he couldn't feel any pain. His heart beat wildly.

"Nah. I'm alright. Can I buy your beautiful daughter an ice cream cone? It's been a tough afternoon. Maybe even one for you?"

Julia looked at this man she once knew. Something was different about him. Something special. He now had a glow of goodness about him.

All three of them walked through the police and crowd to get ice cream. And into a new life together.

The Angel of Death smiled. It was the first time she had ever played matchmaker. It would also be the last. Yes, she would successfully come for Fredrick Simms again — just not for another 50 years.

Thank God it's Monday.

I know. Saying that makes me weird. But I'm not giving up 1/7th of my life being grumpy that it's Monday. I'm also declaring war on fear. Monday is as good a day to do it as any. Because I've seen what fear does. It is toxic. It tears up relationships and hurts those who love you. Fear is the devil walking this Earth. It leads to selfishness which leads to loneliness. Nope. Not allowing fear to rule my life anymore. Get lost, fear. You're not needed anymore.

Monday is a great day to start with a positive outlook. A good place to start would be to be thankful for the blessings in my life. My wife. My kids. My family. I'm grateful for opening my eyes this morning. I am healthy and happy. I had food to eat and a roof over my head. And I have opportunity. I've been given another chance. A chance to use my talents. A chance to lift up the lives of others. And it doesn't have to be some grand, giant gesture. You can defeat fear with 1,000 small acts of kindness.

I'm going to take today to work on forgiveness. That's a big, big bite to take on a Monday morning. But I refuse to have chains of anger wrapped around me anymore. I'm not going to be held prisoner by someone else's fear. On this Monday, I break free of the bonds of anger. And I know the key is to forgive those who I think have wronged me. Even if they know they have!

Yup, It's Monday morning. The sun is out and the sky is a brilliant cobalt blue. I am sitting here counting my blessings — I may not have enough time! And I am going to be thankful for my challenges. They are just opportunities dressed up in ugly clothing. I'm so amazingly blessed.

Thank God it's Monday.

YES, I'M SPYING ON YOU AND YES, YOU'RE BORING.
The JOY of CATS
NSA
U.S. GOV'T
MARSHALL RAMSEY

Larry Gild's D-Day

The gray sea looked like glass to the horizon. A terrible storm had hit this coast 71 years ago. Now all that remained were the salty tears on Lucy Gilds' cheeks.

She gingerly made her way down the path from the bluff to the sea. Her journey was simple compared to her father's. But she wasn't dodging bombs and bullets as he did. Going to the sea was easier than coming from it.

Pvt. Lawrence Gild had done it on a Higgins Boat. Spray and vomit stung his face. Lead killed his friends. Blood stained his clothes. He came ashore on Omaha Beach during the second wave. He was near the tip of the spear on D-Day.

Lucy hadn't known it until March 15, 2015. Her jaw dropped when the lawyer read his final request. Now she was honoring it.

She knew he had served in the Army during the war but thought he was behind the lines. At least that was what her mother said. Her mother was a woman full of secrets.

While she loved her father, she knew her mother's heart belonged to someone else. She had met and fallen in love with a young Marine named Skip Walker.

Lucy had found their yellowed love letters while playing in the attic as a little girl. She sat against a rafter and read his last letter. He was fighting on an island somewhere in the Pacific. While her father was storming ashore on Omaha Beach, a Japanese sniper ended Skip's life.

Part of her mother died that day. The rest died in 1968 when the men in uniform showed up at their front door.

Her brother, a Marine (she remember her father's anger he hadn't joined the Army), was shot in the head by a Viet Cong sniper (how cruel that had to be to her mother). She and her parents stood in the cemetery as cold rain fell around them. The moment his coffin entered the earth, her mother stopped talking and started crying. Her mother would cry as her father sat at the kitchen table holding a glass of scotch.

Cancer took her a year later. But Lucy knew that it was a broken heart that had killed her mother. Her father never remarried. A dark chill fell upon their house.

The Greatest Generation was a tortured one.

Lucy had always thought her father to be cold and unloving. Now she knew the truth. Now she knew demons were haunting him.

Demons born on this beach.

After the war, her father came home, went to school on the G.I. Bill and became a teacher. Mild mannered Larry Gild. Her father retired in 1985 as superintendent of schools. Dementia slowly stole him from her in the late 2000s.

He died in his sleep at the age of 91.

Sleep. That was when the demons normally came. She remembered the screaming she and her brother had heard from his bedroom. Her father, like so many of his generation, dealt with it by swallowing it. He suffered from what was now known as PTSD.

Lucy took her shoes off and felt the sand beneath her feet. She quickly crossed the beach (something her father was not able to do) and walked into the surf. There she opened a small container and pulled out a bag of ashes.

Tears hit the water as the ashes touched the sea. After a lifetime of war, her father finally found peace.

Janitor Chronicles No. 2

My mop glided quietly across the tile floor. I had a method of hitting two rows of squares at a time, thus making my work go by quickly. I still had a couple of classrooms to mop. It was 8:30 p.m. — three hours until quitting time.

Pope High School resembled a tomb. The kids were gone and all who remained in the building were the custodial staff. I was the newest member and fresh out of college. I quickly learned that mopping should be done close to the end of the day. You didn't want people walking across your work.

I wrung out my mop and continued my work.

Suddenly a man turned the corner and walked right down the middle of my work.

"Um, sir," I protested, "the floor is wet!"

The guy looked down his nose at me and said, "So? You're just a janitor. You can re-mop it."

I should have stuck the mop handle up his butt, but instead I just stood there and stared. How dare he talk to me that way?

Jackass.

I heard his voice for days. "You're just a janitor." I wasn't "just a janitor." I was a recent honors graduate from college. I was an award-winning cartoonist. I was… I stopped and thought for a moment: I realized I'm not my job. But how I do my job is a reflection of who I am.

It was one of the most important lessons I ever learned.

Today, editorial cartoonists are going the way of the passenger pigeon. I've seen several of my peers lose their careers entirely. And when their jobs went away, they sank into depression. They were their jobs. Knowing that I'm not a job title gives me strength in uncertain times.

I'm not just an editorial cartoonist. Or a speaker. Or an author. Or a radio host. Or a…

I am who I am. The rest reflects that.

I could easily end up mopping floors again at Pope High School. If I do, I hope that guy walks down my floor again. First I'll thank him. He led me to the most important advice of my career. And then I'll stick the mop handle where the sun don't shine — just because.

The Traveler of Bethlehem

Fatigue gestured to the traveler, pulling him toward it and a certain death. Thank goodness for the road's rumble strips, he thought, or he would have left the road and hit a tree. He needed to find a hotel and quick. But the rural Pennsylvania countryside offered nothing but darkness and trees.

The traveler had rolled down the windows and blasted the radio in a vain attempt to stay awake. Cold air did battle with a certain death. Sleep would be so easy now. So comfortable. Yet, so final.

It was Christmas Eve and he was trying to make his way home. His final flight from Philadelphia had been cancelled due to a sudden snowstorm and he had rented the last car in the airport. The traveler had fought the blizzard for nearly 60 miles until he finally made it to the outskirts of Bethlehem, Pennsylvania. Making it the last 50 miles home seemed like an impossibility. Ice and fatigue were fighting in tandem to stop him. He so wanted to see his boys wake up to find Santa had come. No, he wanted his sons to wake up and find he had arrived. The snow had tapered off and the roads were fairly clear now. The traveler pressed on but knew he needed to sleep.

Now he was just praying for a motel so he could rest his weary head.

Fatigue tugged at him again as his car left the road. The traveler woke up just in time to miss a bridge support. He was awake now. And fear was his co-pilot and was screaming in his ear.

"God, I need a miracle."

When he finished his prayer, he saw a glow in the distance. The traveler sped toward it and saw a sign for a cheap motel. It beckoned him like a flame would a moth. Salvation was on the horizon.

The traveler pulled his small rental Ford into the motel parking lot. It was full. This was worrisome, he thought. He remembered a recent trip across Texas where all the motels all across West Texas had no vacancy. He had ended up driving through the night before making El Paso. Not tonight. He couldn't go another mile further. "God, please let there be a room."

An elderly man sat at the counter, reading an old *Sports*

Illustrated and fighting sleep himself. The traveler carried his bag and asked, "Got a room?"

The innkeeper, hired more for his willingness to work the night shift than for his sterling personality, grunted, "One. You're in luck."

The traveler was relieved. It was his own personal Christmas miracle. He had cheated fatigue for most of the night and now had made it safely to a bed. His credit card made a smart snap as he plunked it down on the counter.

Just then, the doors to the hotel flew open. A man and a very pregnant woman burst through them, carrying two bags. The woman was crying and the man was trying to comfort her by saying, "I'm sure they have a room, honey. I'm sure. If not, we can sleep in the barn behind the hotel."

The traveler stood, looking at the couple and gripping his key. Maybe he could slip out of sight and they wouldn't see him. He did make it there first after all. And he was so tired. Very tired. But as he heard the woman sob louder, he looked at her and sighed. "Oh alright," he mumbled as he walked back to the counter.

"You can have my room," he said to the young man as he handed him his key, "My treat." The young man looked at the traveler and said, "thank you, sir."

The traveler grabbed a pillow and a blanket and as he headed back out to his car, he said, "Merry Christmas." He'd catch a quick snooze and then head on back home in time for Christmas morning.

As he got as comfortable as he could in a rented Ford, the traveler thought about the young couple and smiled. Sleep's angel wrapped her arms safely around him as a bright star illuminated the traveler of Bethlehem.

Humor > Fear

My phone buzzed on the way to work yesterday. I looked down and it was a message from one of the local TV reporters. She had a question for me. Well, I had no idea what she wanted so I turned the radio to the news.

And I promptly found my answer.

Terrorists had slaughtered 12 and wounded 20 at a French satirical publication in Paris, France. And among the 12 were four cartoonists. They had been murdered because the terrorists did not like what they drew. They had been slaughtered because they had dared to express their opinion.

Damn.

The reporter asked me if I was afraid. Good question, I guess. I mean, four cartoonists died. And Lord knows I've made enough people mad over the years. But then I thought, "no." Because you can't live life afraid. You can be shot just taking the trash to the curb. We can stumble across monsters at any time. But that doesn't mean we run away. We can't be locked in fear. We can't live that way — at least for long. And people around the world agree. The outpouring by freedom-loving people yesterday was nothing short of inspiring.

As I was drawing, I thought about the slain cartoonists. And then I thought how police or soldiers must feel when one of their brethren dies. I felt mad, outraged and a little worried. "Would it be me?" Pretty normal emotions, actually.

Then the person at the front desk came to tell me, "Someone's here to see you and they have a camera."

I quipped, "At least it's not a gun."

I used humor to diffuse fear. That's what humanity does. And that's something terrorists will never be able to stop.

Je suis Charlie.

Pip's Restaurant Reviews
While the food has a good flavor, the presentation leaves much to be desired.
PIP
MARSHALL RAMSEY

Powerball

"34 79 23 6 12 and Powerball 7."

Kris Kaylor sat in his pickup truck on the edge of the Natchez bluff. He listened intently while a man read the winning power ball numbers. His hands holding the ticket shook as a cold chill went down his spine. In the past 30 seconds, his life had just changed.

He had won the $500 million Powerball lottery jackpot.

There, on the banks of the Mississippi River, an out-of-work factory worker was now one of the wealthiest men in Mississippi. He felt his heart race. He knew one thing, though: No one could find out. Ever. Not even his extended family. And he knew what he had to do next.

Kris Kaylor had a plan.

Two weeks later, he claimed the jackpot anonymously. He immediately quit his job at the MiniMart, put his trailer up for sale and moved to Oxford, Mississippi.

He had always loved Ole Miss as a kid, even though he knew he could never afford to go there. Now he lived two blocks off the Square in a small condo paid for with cash.

The next thing he did was to enroll in Ole Miss' College of Business. Kris had seen too many lottery winners go broke soon after they had won. It was time for him to learn about his money and how to harness it.

His new-found fortune was like the river he had grown up with; he knew he could quickly drown in it.

Kris soon befriended his accounting professor, Dr. Bob Dollarhyde. One afternoon, he went to Dr. Dollarhyde's office and revealed his secret to him.

As he sat across from his professor, he said, "I've read that you're the best. I need your help. I'll pay you — but really need some advice on how to set some things up."

Dr. Dollarhyde sat there stunned. He then stammered. "OK." And from that moment on, accounts were set up. Income began to stream.

And Kris' immense wealth quietly multiplied.

Jenni Frise was a first-generation college student from Eupora, Mississippi. The daughter of factory workers, she realized that education was her ticket to a better life than that of her parents. But it was expensive. Her tuition was rising like South Delta floodwaters, threatening to wash her dreams away. Brunette with glasses, she wiped her eyes as she sat in the coffee shop on the Oxford Square. A nice man served her coffee and said, "Everything OK?" The girl, stressed out over school and her finances, unloaded on a total stranger.

"NO! I have dreams of becoming an accountant. But I'm going to have to drop out. My mother lost her job last week and my dad is worried about his job. I can't afford to stay here."

The waiter put her coffee down and said, "What's your name?"

The girl, a bit put off by the stranger's request, told him anyway. "Jennifer. Jennifer Frise. My friends call me Jenni."

The man smiled and said, "Don't worry Jenni; things will be OK."

Jenni wiped her nose and thanked the kind man. Little did she know her life was about to be changed, too.

The waiter walked back into the kitchen and made a phone call, "Doc, this is Kris, we have our first winner. Contact the bursar's office and pay Jennifer Frise's tuition until she graduates."

An older couple sat in the booth in the back. The woman was crying as the husband held her hand.

Kris brought them some coffee and slowly walked past but remained within earshot.

"I'm sorry honey. I know what the doctor said but we can't afford the treatment for me. I'm going to make sure you are well taken care of after I die." The woman burst into sobs immediately.

Kris walked back into the kitchen and asked his manager, "Do you know them?"

"Yes," his boss said, "Edna and Frank Marsella. They live a couple of blocks off the Square in a small cottage. Good people. Donate a lot of volunteer time to the school and to Oxford." Kris thanked his boss and walked out of earshot. He picked up his smartphone and once again called a familiar number.

"Yes, call Ed at the hospital and make sure Frank Marsella's treatment is paid for."

A few minutes later, Kris watched as Frank answered his

cellphone. He saw him pause and then drop the phone. Kris picked up dirty dishes three tables away and smiled.

Judy Bowen was a single-mom with two kids. She had left after her husband Billy Jack had beat her nearly unconscious.

She was a woman of great courage and now was desperately trying to rebuild her life by taking night classes at Ole Miss.

But she lacked the funds and the energy to go on. And now that it was Christmas, she was faced with a terrible choice: Rent or Christmas.

She looked at the waiter and said, "Did you ever just want to give up?"

Kris smiled and said, "Only on days that end with Y."

Judy grinned at the joke. "No, seriously. My kids are so good but there won't be a Christmas for them this year."

Kris said, "Why not?"

Judy unloaded her story on the nice man bringing her a cup of coffee. Kris sat down and said, "I know how I can help." Judy looked at him suspiciously but then he said, "I'll buy your coffee today."

Judy laughed. And when she got home from class that night, she found $500 in an envelope with a note that read, "Buy your kids some presents. Santa."

And in a way, Kris Kaylor did become Santa. He quietly found ways to use his new-found fortune to help others. To bring gifts to good people.

He developed a network to find those in need and then paid a tuition bill here, helped with a house note there. And over the next five years, he assisted over 2,000 people. All quietly. All anonymously.

Everyone in Oxford just knew him as the kind man who worked in the local coffee shop. Everyone except two people. One was his best friend, Dr. Bob Dollarhyde. And the other was his new wife, Judy Bowen.

The day she married the nice coffee-shop waiter, she learned her kids would never have to worry about Christmas presents again.

Late one Christmas Eve, Kris looked at his sleeping wife and realized he had truly won life's lottery after all. It wasn't about the money. It was what he was now able to do to help others. He paid his good fortune forward. And as Oxford's secret Santa drifted off to sleep, Kris dreamed of his winning numbers:

"34 79 23 6 12 and Powerball 7."

A Good Dog

It has been a couple of years since our beloved dog Banjo died, but his spirit lives on. It lives when I get a note from a parent telling me how much his or her child loves my book *Banjo's Dream*. It lives when I see a picture of a child reading it. It lives because I know he's still hard at work doing what he did best — loving everyone around him. Sometimes kids ask me about his death and I say, "Banjo's not here anymore but he's right here," and I point to my heart. Because that's where he will forever live. Banjo comforted me when I was at a low point in my life. Like a good dog, he stood by me as I dusted myself off and started dreaming again. I love hearing kids say, "I'm going to dream like Banjo." That's who my old farty brown dog was. He was the little dog who could.

I don't think it was a coincidence that Pip was born at the same exact moment Banjo died. She hasn't filled the hole left in our hearts when Banjo left. No, she created her own spot. It would be easy to compare her to him — but I don't because she's definitely her own dog. I do think, however, she was sent at the exact moment she was needed. And in that, she has done her job well. She makes us laugh, yell, chase her and curse. She answers only to "treat" and steals socks. She has sucked up to my wife and sleeps pressed up against the back of her legs. Pip is an alpha dog who thinks SHE is in charge. And at times, she is. (I don't call her "Queen Bossypants" for nothing.) As I get more comfortable with her personality, I'll be able to write in her rather loud voice.

Never underestimate the healing power of a good dog. They listen when no one else does. They greet you like you've liberated Paris every time you come home. They love you when you're unlovable. DOG spelled backwards is GOD. A good dog will remind you of that every single day.

Thank you, Banjo and Pip, for your spirit and for bringing joy into my family's lives.

The Fortune Teller

New Orleans was the last place James Gibson wanted to be.

While he spoke fluent French, Laissez les bons temps rouler meant nothing to him. He was a man of discipline — A man who stuck to his plan. He didn't believe in debauchery, voodoo, alcohol or any other of the various vices offered along Bourbon Street. Who had time for fun? That night, when his fellow Navy SEAL squad mates went partying, they beckoned, "Come on, old man!" He responded by going to bed.

The alarm greeted him rudely right at sunrise. He laced up his running shoes and left the old hotel. The streets in the French Quarter were wet from the street sweepers who had attempted to erase the evidence from the night before. New Orleans was a city that engaged all five of one's senses. James could smell the spilled drinks from the revelers the night before. He had reluctantly agreed to come over here for the weekend after drills near the Stennis Space Center. As he stretched, he saw the tourists heading toward the Cafe Du Monde to get their sugary fried thingies fix. The powered sugar reminded him of the cocaine factory he had once blown up in Columbia. Overweight men and women marched past Jackson Square to get their fried dough.

James had mixed feelings about New Orleans. It was the city of his birth — but he didn't know his birth parents. They had put him up for adoption when he was born. His adoptive parents — his real parents in his mind — lived in Baton Rouge. So that was his home. He had graduated with honors from LSU and entered the Navy after successfully completing Naval ROTC. His focus, his drive, his pain pushed him harder than all the other officers. BUDS training in San Diego pushed him even harder.

Discipline. Focus. Purpose.

He ran down Decatur Street toward the Convention Center. The relentless humidity reminded him of the jungles of Panama. He ran back up past the National World War II Museum and then looped back toward the French Quarter. James Gibson didn't worry about criminals. Criminals worried about James Gibson.

He had been here after Katrina, providing logistical support for the relief efforts that took too long to get here. He remembered seeing the bodies and the chaos. James would give New Orleans credit for one thing: It was resilient. It earned his respect for that reason and that reason alone.

He ran back down Bourbon and toward Jackson Square. There he saw the artists lined up and saw the fortune tellers in front of the Cathedral. He shook his head. God and Voodoo ten feet apart. As he huffed past, he noticed one lady sitting out on her own. Her handwritten sign read, "Madam Duvall."

"Come over here, boy."

"No offense, ma'am, but I don't believe in fortune telling."

But there was something intriguing about this woman. She seemed familiar.

He sat his sweaty self down in her folding metal chair and she grabbed his palm.

"New Orleans causes you great pain. It digs up many questions in your heart."

OK, this lady was pretty good.

"Many unknowns surround you. Like your parents. You seek your parents."

James pulled his hand back, but Madam Duvall grabbed it and continued on.

"You were given up at birth. You seek your mother. And your mother seeks you."

James was sweating even more, but it wasn't from the heat.

"I can give you answers you seek," Madam Duvall said. "I know who your mother is."

James felt nauseous. He started to stammer and get up but Madam Duvall held up a copy of a piece of paper.

"I, James Gibson, am your mother."

James looked at the woman. She didn't seem much older than he was.

"What?!? No. No, you're not."

She held both his hands and told him the story behind his birth.

"I was 16. Your father and I were in the same high school. He was killed two years later in a gang shooting. I knew I couldn't raise you like you deserved. My mother knew your adoptive parents. Like so many refugees after Katrina, you started a new life in Baton Rouge."

She held out a copy of his birth certificate and a baby picture of him.

James felt a wave of emotion crash over him. Tourists walking past would have noticed the hulking man holding the fortune teller and weeping.

New Orleans is a town that engages all your senses. And on that muggy morning in Jackson Square, a man of great discipline learned the true meaning of love, sacrifice and redemption.

At the End of Our Days

I'm up to my neck today in alligators, but I just wanted to chime in with a little observation. I've watched two people at the end of their lives. One had a million friends. One was selfish. The one with the friends was carried across the finish line by those friends. The selfish one died alone.

I get the concept of self-preservation. But we're put on this Earth to love and serve others. Be grateful for your friends. And be a friend to them. It doesn't have to be grand gestures — just show that you care.

Yazoo City's Zig Ziglar had it right: "You can have everything in life you want, if you will just help enough other people get what they want."

I will read and try to live this for the rest of my life.

THE PAST TENSE OF "WOO" IS "WED."
Z
AMY

A Dog's Life

Cataracts cloud my eyes and scars cover my body. My joints hurt and I move slowly now. The years have stripped me of both youth and energy. As I lie here on the couch, I realize my life is now in the rearview mirror. I'm old now and have gone by many names. But wisdom has permeated my soul.

My dad was a traveler I never knew. My mother, bless her soul, was a small terrier mix. From her, I got my white coat and my incredible will to live. I was born on a farm in a box under a trailer on a very cold Christmas night. Mother cradled us gently as the stars burned brightly in the inky black sky. It was one of the few peaceful times I would know.

Soon after we were born, a human put us in a box and threw us in the back of a truck. I don't remember much from that day, but I know we were dropped off far from the trailer. I recall fleeting images of the rusty, red truck and my mother barking wildly as it rode away. She then did something totally unexpected: She leapt from the truck to be with us.

My mother was amazing like that. She chose us over the humans who betrayed her litter.

She pulled us out of the box and dragged us into the nearby woods. After that, my childhood was a blur of trashcans and handouts. When I was one, mom was hit by a car and left to die in the middle of the highway. The world lost a loving soul when she passed. As we walked away, my brother, sister and I were left to fend for ourselves in a very cruel world.

If you will excuse me, I need to pause for a moment.

One morning, the three of us were approached by a human with a noose on a pole. My brother couldn't escape the noose and was dragged off to a truck. My sister and I watched as it drove off. We never saw our brother again — I hope he is in a better place. My sister and I soon separated after that day. I haven't seen her again either. I pray she found peace as well. She was a kind soul like our mother.

The following fall, a farmer trapped me in a cage near his hen house. I had developed a keen taste for eggs and for some reason, he wasn't willing to share them with me. He was a big, burly man with a prominent scar across his right cheek. He claimed that man was on the top of the pecking order and used

Genesis as an excuse to beat me often and horribly. I was kept chained out in the backyard and subjected to the horrible storms of spring. One night, a horrible thunderstorm rocked the farm. Lightning lit the land like a strobe light. A loud noise, almost like a pulsing jet engine came out of the darkness. The monster raked across the farm — The farmer's house disappeared in a cloud of shrapnel. When morning came, the landscape was littered with dead horses, cows, chickens and two humans.

I guess karma caught up with the farmer's meanness.

I knew I had to leave to survive. So I yanked on the chain to pull the stake out of the moist soil. I put that farm behind me as I drug the chain down the road behind me. One afternoon, I was poking through a bag of trash when I heard a loud explosion. Pain seared through my body as bird shot tore into my side and left leg. The chain jingled as I ran as fast as I could from the second explosion. I curled up in a dark hole, licking the blood from my matted white fur. Pain choked me and as I faded, I saw my mother's beautiful face. I felt a peace like I've never felt before.

I awoke as the human lifted me up. He was gray-headed and wrinkled, but had a warm kindness to his face. I was afraid, but too weak to run. I just whimpered as he carefully laid me on the towel in the cab of his truck and whispered to me that I would be OK. I think he was an angel, although he really didn't look like my mother. I faded again and was blanketed in velvety blackness.

My eyes opened to see steel bars. I can't really describe the smell — it seemed like disinfectant and bleach. There were other animals in cages: A tabby cat. A three-legged terrier who said his name was "Lucky." There was a one-eyed German Shepherd named Hans. I looked at my battered body and saw I was bandaged. The man who had saved me walked into the room and peered down into my cage.

"Hello, my little friend; you've had quite an exciting adventure."

I initially cowered in the back of the cage, but the soothing sound of his voice comforted me. Maybe this human was different. Maybe I wasn't about to get savagely beaten. I walked to the bars and licked his outstretched hand. Salt. So this is what an angel tasted like.

I gathered strength and learned to walk again. Hans told me

we were in what was called a "veterinarian clinic," but I just knew it was different from any other place I had been before. The food was good and the care was loving. I felt a warmth that I had only felt from my mother. Maybe there were good humans out there — yet, I still had my doubts.

And then I met her.

She was blonde, about six years old and full of joy. She bounded into the office and yelled, "GRANDPA." The gray-headed man stopped and picked up the little girl. He called her Anna Grace as he swung her around. The world seemed brighter with her in the room.

"Here's the one I was telling you about, Anna Grace."

I wagged my tail as she came up to me. She dropped to her knees and I jumped up on her.

"I'll call him "Snowball!"

As her mother and father put me into their car, I allowed that to sink in. My name is now Snowball.

I'm old now. I think of all the hardships in my life. I also think of my beloved mother. In my heart, I feel her's beating. I know someday I'll see her and my siblings again. I'm scarred by man's cruelty and yet have survived because of his kindness. But right now, I'm going to doze in Anna Grace's lap.

I'm a dog. And I've led an amazing life.

The Mighty Saturn

It stands as tall as a 36-story building and if it had failed at launch, the explosion would have rivaled a small atomic bomb. It was designed using pencil, paper and sweat by some of the men who had designed the very rockets that had rained down on London during World War II. It lifted off slowly toward the heavens and its 1960s technology never failed (something my 1969 Firebird did occasionally.) It was American's technological miracle. It was the Saturn V.

The Saturn V was — and still is — the most powerful rocket ever built. It took men to the Moon, put Skylab into orbit and lifted our dreams toward the stars. Three exist today — in Huntsville, Alabama (a testing model) and in Florida and Houston, Texas (from cancelled Apollo missions after America became bored with moon missions and Congress didn't want to pay for them). It was replaced by the Space Shuttles — which now reside in museums, too. Someday the massive SLS rocket will rival it. Someday.

But for now, the Saturn V is the king of rockets. And to me, it stands for something even bigger than its giant size.

America had vision back then. We dared to conquer the impossible — and did. The Apollo missions provided hope during a hopeless time. As I stood beneath the mighty rocket this weekend, awed by its size and the size of the dream that created it, I remembered what we are capable of when we pull together. It was when a dream could conquer bureaucracy.

I walked the length of the old rocket and looked at my sons. I can only hope their generation has the courage to dream again like the creators of the Saturn V once did.

3...2...1...liftoff.

Superheroes Don't Wear Capes

Grandpa had said the house had survived Camille. But Grandpa wasn't here fighting for his life -- He was safely in his grave. Caught in the middle of Hurricane Katrina, Linda Grambling was trying desperately to avoid hers.

Katrina's storm surge was crushing Camille's records and the seaside homes in Linda's Waveland neighborhood. Brown water swilled as the wind howled.

"So this is Hell?" Linda thought as she thrashed her arms in the surf. Fire ants landed on her face and bit her.

She had made it to her home's second floor before it collapsed. Her face was pressed against the ceiling when the walls crumbled. This was no way to die. Fatigue in her body burned like the ant bites on her face. She washed toward the railroad tracks -- although she really couldn't tell. The water continued to rise and push her inland. It looked like Noah's worst nightmare.

"Omigod," she feared, "I'll get sucked out to sea if I don't drown first."

"Where's Superman?" she thought. "Where's Batman? Anyone? I need a superhero."

She grabbed onto an oak limb and held onto it as tightly as she could. Her legs wrapped around the tree as she prayed it would hold. The current ripped at her clothes and boards battered her body.

Safe for the moment, Linda closed her eyes.

"Where's Superman?" she thought. "Where's Batman? Anyone? I need a superhero."

Slowly, the sea tired of its assault of the land and retreated back to the Mississippi Sound. Linda, exhausted, passed out.

She awoke to tomb quiet. And then a faint hiss from what sounded like a gas line. There were no birds or bugs. She heard a faint "Help," in the distance. She then heard it again. It was a male voice. "Help, my wife needs help."

"Where's Superman?" she thought. "Where's Batman? Ironman? Anyone?"

She carefully shimmied down the tree. When she got to the final limb it broke, sending her tumbling to the ground. Her body hit hard on top of a pile of boards. Nails impaled her hand and foot. She felt Christ's pain.

The land smelled like salt water, wet wood and death. She had no idea what time it was: Her watch had been ripped off her. So had her shirt. She felt around and at least had her pants and bra on. She would have died of embarrassment otherwise.

"Help!" The cries grew fainter. And then they were replaced with another noise. More voices. This time deeper and stronger: "Hello?!? Anyone alive?"

"OVER HERE!" she responded.

Two figures approached her from North. She looked at them and saw her cries had been answered. Superman and Batman walked toward her!

She reached out her hand to her superheroes and then saw who they really were.

They were a Waveland police officer and a paramedic. Both were battered. But both were there to help.

"Don't worry ma'am, you'll be OK."

As they helped her to her feet, she knew that the superheroes of Katrina didn't wear capes.

When Things Get Bad, We Get Good

The Southeast faced a grim tornado forecast. And we were in its crosshairs.

How grim? Storm chaser Reed Timmer arrived with all three of his Dominator chase vehicles, tornado filmmaker Sean Casey cruised near Tupelo, Jim Cantore mentioned Mississippi repeatedly and Jackson's Weather Channel Tor Con number was a nine out of 10. I wouldn't have been surprised to see the Four Horsemen of the Apocalypse cruising down I-55.

Unfortunately, the forecast was right. April 28, 2014, turned out to be a bad day. A very bad day. A day that carved its name into the record books with a deadly combination of brutal wind, rain and blood.

Louisville, Tupelo, Brandon, Richland, Pearl, Gluckstadt, Canton, Lake Caroline and Vicksburg all suffered damage. Every time a thunderstorm would form, it would drop a long-track, wedge tornado. We watched helplessly as radar-indicated hook echoes stalked our towns. Television meteorologists barely got time to take a breath (when they weren't having to run for cover themselves). We ducked and covered. We prayed. It was a day when Mother Nature showed us who's boss.

As dawn broke on Wednesday, the true scope of the damage raised its ugly head: The blown-out Winston County Medical Center. Bob Boyte Honda's collapsed roof. Damage to homes and businesses in north Tupelo. The crumpled mobile home park in Pearl. Roofs in Lake Caroline peeled off. Cars tossed like toys. Trees snapped. Steel bent. Homes destroyed. And tragically, precious lives lost.

We go through life dumb and happy until a storm like this punches us in the mouth. Days like that Tuesday remind us that our lives can change in a heartbeat.

Mississippi took a beating. A very bad one. But before the sky could clear, we did what we always do. We began helping each other recover.

We did it after Hurricane Katrina. We did it during the Mississippi River flood. We did it after the Smithville and Yazoo City tornados.

I've joked that before you can crawl out of the rubble, there will be a church van full of people with chainsaws and casseroles. There's a lot of truth to it. It's why we're constantly the most generous state. It's one area where we have empathy. We know disaster and how to recover from it.

Today, the pictures in the newspapers, online and on television look grim. Lives and wreckage are scattered randomly on the ground. But the healing has already begun. We're donating food and clothing. We're giving blood. We're helping with the clean-up. Checks are being written. Friends and family are being lifted up. We'll get through this disaster. We always do. Because while we're powerless in the face of nature, we're very powerful when it comes to compassion.

People around the country sometimes challenge me to say something good about Mississippi. My answer? Compassion in the face of disaster.

That's because in Mississippi, when things get bad, we get good.

MIKE, MIKE MIKE!! GUESS WHAT DAY IT IS?!
MAKE. HIM. STOP!!

463747
FT
Charlotte's Chariot II
2015

The Knight's Final Flight

Snap. Crackle. Pop.

Arthritic knees creaked as the old man climbed onto the wing. This had been so much easier 70 years ago, he thought, as he carefully slid into the open cockpit of the P-51D Mustang fighter plane. Air and familiar smells filled his scarred lungs.

With eyes closed, he saw a war from long ago.

To his right sat his old helmet. It fit snuggly on his balding head. He adjusted his glasses and scanned all the instruments.

Just like riding a bike.

Two brown eyes stared back at him from the instrument panel. It was the beautiful face of his beloved late wife. He remembered when he had tacked the picture there on that dark day in France. Her love got him through the hard times: During the war — and for the next 60 years. He knew he'd see her soon.

He flipped a couple of switches and the powerful Rolls Royce Merlin engine roared to life. It pulsed like the heartbeat of a lion. The Mustang was one of the premier fighters of World War II and he was one of the knights who flew it. Soaring through the skies over Europe, he had drawn blood twice and had shared credit for a third kill. Today's flight would be more peaceful. No German ME-109s or flak. Just pink and white cloud tops.

The engine roared louder as he pushed the throttles forward. His heartbeat climbed with the tachometer. He checked the ailerons and rudder.

Cleared for take off.

As the plane rolled down the runway, he felt his body press into the seat. Few mortals could understand this kind of power. Faster, faster, faster -- the plane leapt off the ground. You didn't push the throttle of a Mustang all the way forward on takeoff because of the engine's massive torque and giant propeller. He had seen fellow pilots actually flip their plane doing that. But once he was in the air, he slipped the throttle forward, pulled back on the stick and shot into the sky like a rocket.

The world seemed unusually vibrant. He saw a flock of white egrets flying above the bright green earth. Houses looked like toys. Earthly concerns faded as did his aches and pains. He banked the Mustang and flew West into the sun.

That's when he saw them. There were three other Mustangs

flying in formation off to the South. For some reason, his radio wasn't working, but when they saw him, they joined up on his wing. It was 1945 all over again.

Below was a group of cars. Nearby a crowd of people in black surrounded a tent. The formation of Mustangs roared overhead and then circled back around for another pass. The old man led the formation and then shot skyward solo as they performed the missing man formation.

The other Mustangs formed back on his wing and the pilots individually saluted him. When he noticed his fuel gauge nearing empty, he saluted back and peeled off from the formation.

It was time to head home.

Fog shrouded the runway. White wisps tickled the asphalt's black linear shape, giving it a mystical look. Flaps down. Gear down. Throttle back. The ground welcomed him. The Mustang couldn't have been running any better.

Screech. Screech.

Two puffs as rubber met asphalt. Fog embraced him, making visibility difficult. He pointed the Mustang's nose toward the bright light ahead.

As the Mustang fell silent, the old man threw open the cockpit. He could feel the cool moisture blanket him. He heard a familiar voice call out to him.

"You're home!"

Through the mist, a familiar figure ran toward his plane. It was his wife -- just as she looked in the photo. He looked in his plane's mirror and saw the World War II version of himself.

He hopped pain-free off the wing and into the arms of the love of his life. He turned around and looked at his beloved Mustang.

It had taken him home one last time.

– In memory of Cary Salter